FRANTIC
ASSEMBLY

A Frantic Assembly and Theatre Royal Plymouth production.

# THE UNRETURNING

## by Anna Jordan

This production of *The Unreturning* was first performed on 20 September 2018 at Theatre Royal Plymouth, before touring the UK.

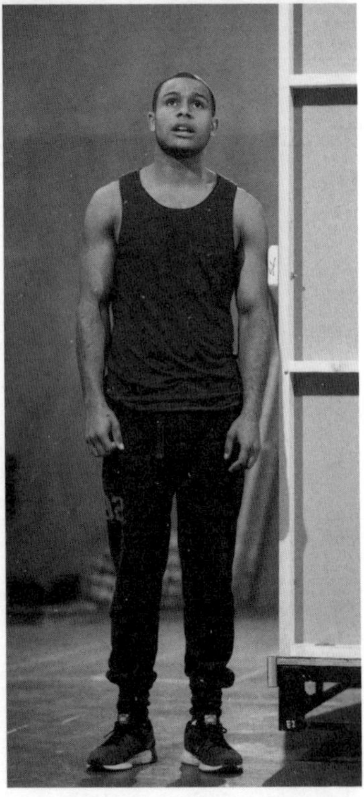

Photography by Helen Maybanks

## CREATIVE TEAM

| | |
|---|---|
| Writer | Anna Jordan |
| Director | Neil Bettles |
| Set and Video Designer | Andrzej Goulding |
| Lighting Designer | Zoe Spurr |
| Sound Designer | Pete Malkin |
| Costume Designer | Lily Arnold |
| Associate Director | Jessica Williams |

## CAST

| | |
|---|---|
| Frankie | Jared Garfield |
| George | Joe Layton |
| Nat | Jonnie Riordan |
| Finn | Kieton Saunders-Browne |

## PRODUCTION TEAM

| | |
|---|---|
| Production Manager | Nick Soper |
| CSM (on book) | Sarah Thomas |
| TSM (Production Manager touring) | Nick Hill |
| Production Video and Sound | Benjamin Walden |
| ASM | Anthony Papamichael |
| Production LX | Matthew Whale |
| Programmer | Lauren Kunicki |
| Video System Engineer | Dan Trenchard |
| Video System Rigger | Michael Samuel |
| Costume Supervisor | Delia Lancaster |
| Drum Technician | Matt Hoyle |

## FOR FRANTIC ASSEMBLY

| | |
|---|---|
| Artistic Director | Scott Graham |
| Executive Director | Kerry Whelan |
| Producer | Peter Holland |
| General Manager | Angie Fullman |
| Head of Learning and Participation | Sharon Kanolik |
| Ignition Project Manager | Juliet Styles |
| Finance and Office Administrator | Gemma Grand |
| Associate Director (Learn and Train) | Simon Pittman |
| Learning and Participation Coordinator | Conor Hunt |

| | |
|---|---|
| **Public Relations** | The Corner Shop / www.cornershoppr.com |
| **Marketing & Sales** | Joe Public / www.joepublicmarketing.com |

**FOR THEATRE ROYAL PLYMOUTH**

| | |
|---|---|
| Chief Executive | Adrian Vinken OBE |
| Artistic Director | Simon Stokes |
| Artistic Associate | David Prescott |
| Producer | Louise Schumann |
| Head of Media and Communications | Anne-Marie Clark |
| Media and Communications Officer | Maia Bishenden |
| Head of Marketing | Phillipa Revest |
| Senior Marketing Officer | Judith Lancaster |
| Education Producer | Ben Vleminckx |

**With thanks to:**

The Globe, Vanessa Sutherland, National Youth Theatre, The Old Diorama, The Playground Theatre, CJ Ashen, Matthew Churcher, Gary Duncan, Calum Gulvin, Ryan Hutton, Kristen Indahl, Sam Johnson, Ishmael Khan, Michael Lynch, Ryan Mackay, Anna Moutrey, Lindo Nkomo, Victor Oshin, Felipe Pacheco, Dan Parr, Karl Queensborough and Max Revel.

## CREATIVE TEAM BIOGRAPHIES

### ANNA JORDAN (WRITER)

Anna Jordan won the 2013 Bruntwood Prize for her play *Yen* after having been twice longlisted for her plays *Marianne* and *Chicken Shop. Yen* has had productions at Manchester Royal Exchange, the Royal Court and MCC New York as well as several international productions. It was also shortlisted for the Susan Smith Blackburn Prize 2015–2016.

Recently, Anna has written *Pop Music* for Paines Plough which will tour in 2018. She has also adapted Bertolt Brecht's *Mother Courage and Her Children* for Headlong which will tour in 2019.

Other theatre writing includes *We Anchor In Hope* (Royal Court Theatre – Beyond the Court); *A Serious Case of the Fuckits* (CSSD); *Chicken Shop* (Park Theatre); *Freak* (Theatre503/Assembly Studios) and *Offliners* (LAMDA).

Writing for TV includes staff writer for *Succession* (HBO), and a pilot of her own drama series on addiction *Cluck* (Little Brother Productions). Film includes *The Ivory Year* (LAMDA).

Anna also directs and teaches acting. She directed Jonathan Harvey's play *Tomorrow I'll Be Happy* at The National Theatre Shed as part of National Theatre Connections. Other directing experience includes *Freak* (Theatre503/Assembly Studios), *3 Winters, Touched* and *The Crucible* (Italia Conti BA Hons); *Earthquakes in London* (Arts Educational BA Hons); *Crystal Springs* (Eureka Theatre, San Francisco); *Only Human, Vote of No Confidence* (Theatre503). She has worked at many London drama schools teaching both acting and playwriting, including RADA, LAMDA, Central, Arts Ed and Italia Conti. She also runs her own company – Without a Paddle Theatre, as well as a support network for recent drama-school graduates called The Long Game. She co-founded Hackney Showroom Young Actors – a free weekly acting training for young people based in Hackney.

### NEIL BETTLES (DIRECTOR)

Neil has worked with Frantic Assembly since 2004.

For Frantic Assembly he directed *This Will All Be Gone* and co-directed *No Way Back* for the company and was Assistant Director of *Dirty Wonderland* at the Brighton Festival.

Other credits include, International Associate Movement Director of *Harry Potter and The Cursed Child* (London, New York and Australia); Associate Director of *We Are Here* (La Mama, New York). As movement director, *Carmen* (Opera Wuppertal, Germany); *The James Plays* (Edinburgh International Festival and National Theatre); *Blood Wedding* and *The Bacchae* (Royal & Derngate). As Associate Movement Director, *Heisenberg* (Wyndham's Theatre); *The Light Princess* (National Theatre), and *The Full Monty* (Sheffield Theatres and West End).

He is co-founder and Artistic Director of ThickSkin for which his directing credits include *Chalk Farm, The Static* and *Blackout*. He also co-directed *Boy Magnet* and *White Noise* for the company.

**ANDRZEJ GOULDING (SET AND VIDEO DESIGNER)**
Andrzej works as a Set and Projection Designer internationally across all forms of live performance.

For Frantic Assembly he was Set and Video designer for *No Way Back*.

Set and Video credits include *Status* (Edinburgh Festival 2018); *People, Places and Things* (National Theatre/West End/St Ann's Warehouse, UK tour); *Groundhog Day* (Broadway/Old Vic); *The Girl on the Train* (West Yorkshire Playhouse); *Pressure* (West End/UK tour/Park Theatre); *Frost/Nixon* (Sheffield Crucible); *Coriolanus* (Donmar Warehouse/NT Live); *1984* (Northern Ballet/Sadler's Wells/Sky Arts); *Kiss of the Spider Woman* (Menier Chocolate Factory); *The Suicide, From Morning To Midnight,* (National Theatre); *Relative Values* (West End); *Me and My Girl, Sweet Bird of Youth, The Boy in the Striped Pyjamas, Pressure* (Chichester Festival Theatre); *No's Knife* (Old Vic Theatre/Abbey Theatre); *Carousel* (Barbican, Opera North); *Rent* (St James Theatre/UK tour 2016–17); *Room* (Theatre Royal Stratford East/Abbey Theatre); *Man To Man* (Edinburgh Festival 2015/BAM/UK tour); *The Machine* (MIF/The Armoury NYC); *Into The Hoods : Remixed* (Peacock Theatre/UK tour); *The Last Mermaid* (WMC); *Rules for Living* (UK tour); *Hansel and Gretel* (Vienna State Opera); *The Impresario / Le Rossignol* (Santa Fe Opera); *Silent Night* (US tour).

Set Designs include *Union* (Lyceum Theatre, Edinburgh) and *Sane New World* (Ruby Wax tour).

He was recently nominated for a Drama Desk Award (for *People, Places and Things*), won the 2017 Theatre and Technology Award for Creative Innovation in Video Design (for *Room*) and was nominated for the first ever Whatsonstage Award for Video Design in 2017 (for *Groundhog Day*).

www.agoulding.com

**ZOE SPURR (LIGHTING DESIGNER)**
Zoe trained at the Royal Central School of Speech and Drama.

Recent theatre includes: *Toast* (Traverse 1); *Meek* (Headlong/UK tour); *Abigail's Party* (Queens Theatre Hornchurch/UK tour); *Polstead* (for Eastern Angles/UK tour); *Sticky, Infinite Joy, Confidence, Natives, Collective Rage* (Southwark Playhouse); *Tiny Dynamite* (Old Red Lion); *The Phlebotomist* (Hampstead Theatre); *Not Talking* (Arcola Theatre); *Grotty* (Bunker Theatre); *Phoenix Rising, Loose Lips* (Big House Theatre Company, site specific); *The Beginners* (Unicorn Theatre); *Elephant* (Birmingham REP); *The Magic Flute* (Soho Theatre/UK tour); *The Scar Test* (Soho Theatre); *Skate Hard Turn Left* (BAC); *The Drive* (UK tour); *Hidden* (UK tour); *Elton John's Glasses, Good Dog* (Watford Palace/UK tour); *Erwartung/Twice Through The Heart* (for Shadwell Opera at Hackney Showroom); *The Knife of Dawn* (Camden Roundhouse) and *Affection* (with Outbox Theatre, site specific)

**PETE MALKIN (SOUND DESIGNER)**
Pete is a multi-award-winning Sound Designer for Theatre and a graduate of the Royal Central School of Speech and Drama.

Sound Designer credits include, *Pity* (Royal Court); *Queens of the Coal Age* (Manchester Royal Exchange); *The Seagull* (Lyric Hammersmith); *The Kid Stays in the Picture* (Royal Court); *Frogman* (Curious Directive); *The White Bike* (The Space); *Schism* (Aegis Productions); *The Tempest* (Donmar Warehouse); *Beware of Pity* (Schaubühne, Berlin/Complicité); *Twelfth Night* (Manchester Royal Exchange); *Treasure* (Finborough Theatre);

*Unearthed* (Arcola/UK tour); *7–75* (The Place); *Am I Dead Yet* (Unlimited/ Bush Theatre); *War Correspondents* (Greenwich Festival/UK tour); *The Commission* (ROH/Aldeburgh/Opera North); *Sun* (St Leonard's Church/ National Art Service); *Farragut North* (Southwark); *Space Junk* (Gameshow /Lyric Hammersmith).

Co-Sound Designer credits include: *The Encounter* (Complicité); *The Noise* (Northern Stage/Unlimited Theatre).

Associate Sound Designer credits include: *Harry Potter and the Cursed Child* (West End/Broadway); *1984* (Headlong); *Oresteia* (West End); *Hamlet* (RSC); *Lionboy, The Magic Flute, The Master & Margarita* (Complicité).

Pete's sound work also includes co-sound designing the UN Global Goals launch and Sydney Opera House *Light the Sails* events.

In 2017 Pete won the Special Tony Award for sound design, with Gareth Fry, for Complicité and Simon McBurney's *The Encounter.*

**LILY ARNOLD (COSTUME DESIGNER)**
Set and costume design credits include: *Things of Dry Hours* (Young Vic); *The Girl on the Train* (West Yorkshire Playhouse); *Dublin Carol* (Sherman Theatre); *Rules for Living* (ETT/Royal & Derngate); *Snow in Midsummer, The Jew of Malta, The Rape of Lucrece, King Lear, The Taming of the Shrew* (Royal Shakespeare Company); *Room* (Stratford East); *The Secret Garden* (York Theatre Royal/Theatre by the Lake); *The Solid Life of Sugar Water* (National Theatre/Theatre Royal Plymouth); *The Sugar-Coated Bullets of The Bourgeoisie* (HighTide/Arcola); *Tomcat* (Southwark Playhouse); *Jeramee, Hartleby and Ooglemore* (Unicorn Theatre); *Forget Me Not* (Bush Theatre); *So Here We Are* (HighTide/Manchester Royal Exchange); *Gruesome Playground Injuries, The Edge of Our Bodies* (Gate Theatre); *Beached* (Marlowe Theatre); *Yellow Face* (Park Theatre/ National Theatre); *Peddling* (HighTide Festival/59E59); *Ahasverus, The Bullet* (Hampstead Downstairs); *A Season in the Congo, The Scottsboro Boys* (Young Vic).

Upcoming productions include, *Love Lies Bleeding* (PRINTROOM); *Sleeping Beauty* (Theatre Royal Stratford East); *The Remains of the Day* (Royal & Derngate).

www.lilyarnolddesign.com

**JESSICA WILLIAMS (ASSOCIATE DIRECTOR)**
Jess trained at the London Contemporary Dance School. On graduating she joined Transitions Dance Company at the Laban Centre.

Jess began working for Frantic Assembly in 2012 as a practitioner and has taught movement at MA level for Frantic Assembly and for the Royal Academy of Music and the Oxford School of Drama.

For Frantic Assembly she toured the UK for *Curious Incident of the Dog in the Night-Time* and went on to become Associate Movement Director for the US touring production of *Curious Incident.* She also performed in *This Will All Be Gone* for the company.

Other credits include Co-Directing for the National Youth Theatre Wales, Associate Movement Director for the National Theatre of Wales, and Movement Director for Dirty Protest. Jess is co-Director of Wales-based bilingual company Neontopia and works as movement director for LA based company Wilderness.

## CAST BIOGRAPHIES

### JARED GARFIELD (GEORGE)

Jared is best known to television audiences for his recurring role as Nathan Nightingale in *Hollyoaks* (C4) from 2015 to 2017. He has also appeared on television in *Dr Who*'s 2017 Christmas Special (BBC) and *Midsomer Murders* (ITV). On film he has appeared in *Boy A* (Cuba Pictures) opposite Andrew Garfield.

Recent theatre credits include: Mr Deville in *A Harlem Dream* (Young Vic); Lysander in Watch Your Head's *A Midsummer Night's Dream* (Windsor Castle); and *The Dishwashers* (Birmingham Rep/UK tour).

### JOE LAYTON (FRANKIE)

Joe trained at Drama Centre and made his stage debut in *A Level Playing Field* (Jermyn Street Theatre).

Joe's television work includes roles in Marvel's *Agents of S.H.I.E.L.D, Tatau, Thirteen* (BBC Three), *Casualty, Father Brown* (BBC) and *New Worlds* (C4).

### JONNIE RIORDAN (NAT)

Jonnie is an actor, director and movement director.

Previous work with Frantic Assembly as a performer includes *This Will All Be Gone* and *No Way Back*, and *Canticles* (Brighton Festival/Aldeburgh Music).

Other acting credits include *Full Stop* (Light The Fuse/Lyric Hammersmith /Greenwich and Docklands International Festival); *The Marriage of Figaro* (Opera Holland Park); *Night Film* (Stand + Stare); *Mortal: A Drama* (Wellcome Collection); and *In His Image* (Hampstead Theatre).

Jonnie is also associate director of ThickSkin, appearing as an actor in their productions *Boy Magnet* and *These Imagined Stories* and directing *Boy Magnet and White Noise*. Other directing credits include: the first stage adaptation of Nigel Slater's *Toast* (The Lowry) and *Found* (The Albany). As movement director his credits include: *Great Apes* (Arcola Theatre); *Connections Festival 16/17* (National Theatre); *Maggie & Pierre* (Finborough Theatre); The Paper Birds' *Mobile* (UK tour); Frozen Light's *Home* (UK tour); *CAUGHT* (Pleasance Theatre); and *Cracking, Hooked* and *Bat Boy* (New Wimbledon Studio).

### KIETON SAUNDERS-BROWNE (FINN)

Kieton trained at the Young Actors Theatre and will be making his professional stage debut in *The Unreturning*. Kieton's film credits include *Pulling* (Kaiser Siren Films) and *The Backseat* (Hidden Art Films).

# FRANTIC ASSEMBLY

Award-winning theatre company Frantic Assembly's method of devising theatre has been impacting theatrical practice and unlocking the creative potential of future theatre-makers for 24 years.

One of the most exciting theatre companies in the UK, Frantic Assembly is led by Artistic Director and co-founder Scott Graham, and has toured extensively across Great Britain, and worked in 40 countries internationally collaborating with some of today's most inspiring artists.

Frantic Assembly is currently studied as leading contemporary theatre practitioners on five British and international academic syllabuses. The success of the company's distinct approach has influenced contemporary theatre-making and foregrounded the use of movement directors and choreographers in new dramatic works. With a history of commissioning writers such as Mark Ravenhill, Abi Morgan, Simon Stephens and Bryony Lavery the company has been acclaimed for its collaborative approach. In 2016 the company started delivering practical modules on a new Collaborative Theatre-Making MA it has created with Coventry University (UK Modern University of the Year 2014, 2015, 2016 and UK University of the Year 2015). Frantic Assembly runs Ignition, a free national training programme for young men aged 16–20, increasing involvement and access to the arts in places of low cultural engagement.

Frantic Assembly productions include *Fatherland*, *Things I Know To Be True* (UK and Australia), *Othello*, *Beautiful Burnout* (UK, Australia, New Zealand and New York), *Lovesong*, *Stockholm* (UK and Australia), *The Believers*. They are also the movement directors on the award-winning Royal National Theatre Production of *The Curious Incident of the Dog in the Night-Time* (West End, Broadway, UK and Ireland tour, US tour, China). Television credits include movement direction on BAFTA-winning British-American series *Humans* (AMC, Channel 4 and Kudos).

Theatre Royal Plymouth

*The Unreturning* is Theatre Royal Plymouth's eighth co-production with Frantic Assembly.

Theatre Royal Plymouth specialises in the production of new plays alongside the presentation of a broad range of theatre – including classic and contemporary drama, musicals, opera, ballet and dance. We have three performance spaces – The Lyric (1300-seat proscenium arch), The Drum (175 capacity flexible studio) and The Lab (50 capacity development studio). Our work with young people and communities is extensive and radical, taking place across all our venues and beyond.

Theatre Royal Plymouth productions include: *49 Donkeys Hanged* by Carl Grose, *Clockwork Canaries* by Christopher William Hill, *The Here and This and Now* by Glenn Waldron, *The War Has Not Yet Started* by Mikhail Durnenkov, *Monster Raving Loony* by James Graham, *The Man With The Hammer* by Phil Porter, *The Whipping Man* by Matthew Lopez, *After Electra* by April de Angelis, *Grand Guignol* and *Horse Piss for Blood* by Carl Grose, *Merit* by Alexandra Wood, *Another Place* by DC Moore, *Chekhov in Hell* by Dan Rebellato, *The Astronaut's Chair* by Rona Munro, *Solid Air* by Doug Lucie, and *MAD MAN* by Chris Goode.

The Theatre Royal Plymouth also collaborates with some of the best artists and theatre-makers in the UK and internationally. We have regularly co-produced with Ontroerend Goed (*£YE$, World Without Us, Are We Not Drawn Onward To New Era, A History of Everything, Sirens, Fight Night*), Paines Plough (*The Angry Brigade* by James Graham, *Love Love Love* by Mike Bartlett), Frantic Assembly (*Othello, The Believers* by Bryony Lavery, *Lovesong* by Abi Morgan) and Told By An Idiot (*Napoleon Disrobed, Heads Will Roll, And The Horse You Rode In On, My Perfect Mind*). South West based theatre company The Wrong Crowd are our first resident company.

We have also co-produced with Complicité (*The Master and Margarita, A Disappearing Number*), Hofesh Shechter (*Sun, Political Mother*), Graeae (*The Solid Life of Sugar Water*) and David Pugh, Dafydd Rogers, Kneehigh Theatre (*Rebecca*) and Jamie Hendry (*Wind in the Willows*, which played the London Palladium). Alongside our own productions we present a programme of quality and popularity and regularly launch national touring productions including *Swan Lake, Edward Scissorhands* and *The Red Shoes* (Matthew Bourne) and *War Horse* (National Theatre).

Chief Executive **Adrian Vinken OBE** | Artistic Director **Simon Stokes** | Marketing & Communications Director **Marianne Locatori** | Operations Director **Helen Costello** | Director of Engagement & Learning **Mandy Precious**



Registered Charity Number: 284545
theatreroyal.com

Supported using public funding by ARTS COUNCIL ENGLAND
John Ellerman Foundation
PLYMOUTH CITY COUNCIL

# FRANTIC IGNITION

Frantic Assembly has always been about more than just our work on stage. It is about the ethos of collaboration, of empowerment, of that constant desire to improve. It is about telling stories in voices we don't always hear and about finding talent in places we don't always look. Over the years the Frantic Method of devising theatre has helped people throughout the world connect and make great work.

Since 2008, Frantic Assembly has delivered Ignition, an innovative, free, vocational training programme for young men aged 16–20 years. This national programme, now celebrating 10 years of impact, works with over 600 young men a year. Following a programme of national outreach workshops and trials, delivered in partnership with regional venues and groups, Frantic Assembly selects 12 young men from across the country who then live and work together in London for an intensive week to create a performance. We specifically target those with little previous experience of, or access to, the arts; for example, BAME young people, those with disabilities and young men from areas of high deprivation.

Ignition is inclusive and accessible with a genuine focus on the development of all of the young people that take part. The performance work produced is authentic and reflects the personalities and varied life experiences of the participants. The process is engaging and inspires a sense of personal progression for each individual.

The cast of *The Unreturning* - Joe, Jared, Jonnie and Kieton - are all past alumni of Ignition and demonstrate the impact and legacy that the programme has. Other previous Ignition company members have gone on to study performance and have successful careers in theatre, TV, film. Several have performed in Frantic Assembly productions and many have trained as practitioners, teaching the Frantic Method world-wide.

In 2019 we will be expanding Ignition and opening up the programme to young women for the first time. This will mean that we can inspire more people and provide more opportunities for them to develop their confidence, skills and aspiration and connect with the theatre industry.

As a free to access programme Ignition requires substantial funding and Frantic Assembly has worked with Trusts and Foundations to help deliver its ambition.  We will continue to invest in this vital activity and welcome any and all support.

If you would like to find out more about how you may be able to help please contact our Executive Director, Kerry Whelan on kerry@franticassembly.co.uk

MATUTU

## DIRECTOR'S NOTE

Back in 2008 when we first launched Ignition, the ambition was to develop young male performers who would potentially be Frantic performers of the future. Ten years on and with over 140 graduates of the project, we get to put our money where our mouth is. A full-scale touring show that has been developed with Ignition graduates and finally cast from the same pool.

Through Ignition we travel the country finding young men who we hope will benefit from our way of making theatre. Young men who may not have found themselves in a theatre before, let alone on stage performing. Having directed all twelve Ignition performances it has been incredible to develop this play with Anna Jordan and various teams of Ignition graduates. We told stories, worked physically, made scenes and eventually landed on a simple idea. What does it mean to return to your home after a life-changing experience? To return home and for your world to feel a little different. Maybe you have changed, or maybe the place you are returning to no longer recognises you.

War was something we talked about a lot, and with the centenary of World War One very present in our thoughts we started to develop stories about how that experience can have a profound effect on the people involved. That is how we find ourselves where we are now. Three young men returning to their hometown of Scarborough in different periods in time: 1918, 2013 and 2026. Anna Jordan has built a complex and poetic play with interwoven stories that imagines three very different reasons to return home. All driven by conflict.

The exciting task has been to find a way for all three stories to exist at the same time in the same space. To be together but worlds apart.

*Neil Bettles*

**TOUR DATES**

THEATRE ROYAL PLYMOUTH
Thu 20 Sep – Sat 6 Oct 2018
www.theatreroyal.com

NUFFIELD SOUTHAMPTON THEATRES CAMPUS
Tue 9 – Sat 13 Oct 2018
www.nstheatres.co.uk

EVERYMAN, LIVERPOOL
Tue 16 – Sat 20 Oct 2018
www.everymanplayhouse.com

TRAVERSE THEATRE, EDINBURGH
Wed 24 – Sat 27 Oct 2018
www.traverse.co.uk

THE OLD REP BIRMINGHAM
Tue 30 Oct – Fri 2 Nov 2018
www.oldreptheatre.co.uk

THEATRE ROYAL STRATFORD EAST
Wed 16 Jan – Sat 2 Feb 2019
www.stratfordeast.com

CHICHESTER MINERVA
Tue 5 Feb – Sun 9 Feb 2019
www.cft.org.uk

LEICESTER CURVE
Tue 12 Feb – Sun 16 Feb 2019
www.curveonline.co.uk

TALIESIN ARTS CENTRE, SWANSEA
Tue 21 Feb – Sat 23 Feb 2019
www.taliesinartscentre.co.uk

OXFORD PLAYHOUSE
Tue 26 Feb – Fri 01 Mar 2019
www.oxfordplayhouse.com

**www.franticassembly.co.uk**

# THE UNRETURNING

Anna Jordan

**Thanks**

Thomas Scurr

Ben Newton

Tim Briggs

Karan Gill

Sam Newton

Gareth Morgan

James Tobin

Gary Duncan

Dan Parr

Ryan Hutton

Victor Oshin

David Hemsted

Chris Urch

Camilla Young

Scott Chaloff

Phone Credit for Refugees Charity

*A.J.*

*For Chris Urch*
*whose support never ends*
*and whose personality never fizzles*

**Characters**

NAT
FRANKIE
GEORGE
OFFICER
ARMY BUDDY ONE
ARMY BUDDY TWO
ARMY BUDDY THREE
ELIAS
TRAFFICKER
KIM
ALDO
ROSE
REBEL
MUM (FRANKIE'S)
DOCTOR
MOTHER (GEORGE'S)
FATHER (GEORGE'S)
TONY
RYAN
LUKE
KET
FINN
DR COHEN
TIBBS
CHORUS (PLURAL)

## Note on Play

Chorus should be played by various members of the company. We should slip seamlessly between scenes with pace.

/ indicates an overlap.

… indicates a trailing-off or a searching for words, but rarely a slowing down.

*This text went to press before the end of rehearsals and so may differ slightly from the play as performed.*

## Prologue

## Longing

NAT. I want to return to my home.

I want to find myself there.
I want to meet myself coming back!
And I'll say to myself – what kept you, dickhead?
I want to greet the landscape! Disappear into it
I won't just look
But I'll touch.
Bury whole limbs in the sand
Lean into the wind
Feel the spray on my face
Salt on my tongue
Nourish my heart.
I want to tear across the Valley Bridge
Heart thumping in my chest
I want to go everywhere we went on our boards
With my brother
The VRcades
The firefight simulators at Luna Park
All will reopen just to greet me.
I want to scan our front door again
Hear that familiar beep and clunk
I want to find the ghosts I'm looking for
Need to find them – flesh and bone
But if I can't?
I'll lie on the floor of every room in Our House.
Face down. Soak up our history from the carpet.
Feed on the past.
And when my heart is full?
I want to leap off the headland in all my clothes.
Enter the water with a violent crash
No Fear!

And then
Silence.

I allow myself to sink.
Watch the bubbles that come from me rise to the light
I'll make my peace with the sea
Childhood fears
And fraught journeys of adulthood
Erased as the North Bay envelopes me
In the dark and the calm – alone
I am Home.

FRANKIE. I want to return to my home.

I want a hero's welcome.
I want fanfares, and parades, and brass bands and
the back room of The Lion? Luke and Ket and Ryan and
banners, and balloons and sausage rolls and Jägerbombs and
Golden Balls Frankie is coming home!
I want to lose myself in the face of my mum. And my sister.
Does that sound gay?
I want to speak to my nan for like a *whole* hour – maybe
more!
Greet the Front Door like an old friend.
Rest my forehead on the cold brick of the garage wall
lie under the skylight on my mum's bed
and watch clouds
I wanna answer the landline!
Run my fingers through the shag pile
Stick my head in the fridge!

I want to go out.
I want to go out out.
Drink and dance and shout for no reason
start in the spoons and end up in Vivaz
lines of coke in the back of an Astra
in a pub car park.
Feel invincible
(*Chants.*) SCAR-BA-DOS!
I want to sing in the streets
And shag lamp posts

And puke in the gutter
(*His tone changes.*) And they will never know
(*Beat.*)
None of them will ever know what I –

I want to run on the sand with my dick out. Salt in my nostrils. Wind in my hair.
I want to brave the waves.
*ROAR* into them:
I OWN THE COAST.
Let them dissolve me. Reduce me to mist and foam.
Let them take me back with them into the dark – forever
A shadow
A creak in the floorboard
Of Home.

GEORGE. I want to return to my home.

I want to drink tea.
Hear the clink of the china and the glug of the pour.
Tea with my kin.
Hot. From a pot.
I want my mother to read my leaves and tell me
'There's nothing to fear, dear George!
Just clear flat roads ahead.'

I want to see Rose.
I want to walk along the front with Rose.
I want to hear her voice.
Make her laugh.
Give her what she wants.
A little version of herself to fall in love with!
A little version of me…
We'll take the cliff lift down to the bay
Catch a show at The Spa
Take a rowboat out to sea
I want to run along the sand
like a kid tearing through back-of-his-hand streets.
For no reason but to feel the wind on my cheeks.
The sting of salt.

I want to be part of something I understand
Good English voices, plump round faces…
Not dark hollows for eyes and open wounds for mouths I want roast beef.

I want to wake in the night shouting for Rose and find she's there.
My wife by candlelight.
I want to smell her carbolic lavender smell.
I want to hide in her petticoats.
I want to rip them.
NO.
I want to protect her.
I'll gather her up in my arms
and hold her in my hands like this, see, my little bird
and squeeze her and squeeze her until her
little bones break.
Tear off her wings.
No!
NO!
PLEASE!

*Beat. He gathers himself.*

I want to be with her
*need* to be with her
she's Home.

## ACT ONE

### Leaving

*Focus:* FRANKIE.

CHORUS *should be more than one voice.*

CHORUS. Frankie sits on the bed.
Sheets stripped, kit neatly folded by his side.
Sarge in the doorway
Can't look him in the eye.
Frankie stands on unsteady legs.
Grabs his bag

*Focus switches to* NAT.

Nat's bag:
Tablet (wrapped in plastic)
Charger (wrapped in plastic)
Glucose tablets
Ibuprofen
Spare pants
Spare socks
Spare plastic!

*An* OFFICER *at a desk with a checklist.* GEORGE *in front of him clutching a bunch of papers. He gives them to him as he asks for them.*

OFFICER. Papers?

CHORUS (*still in* NAT*'s world*). What?

OFFICER. Got your papers, man?

GEORGE. Yes, sir.

*He gives him the forms.*

OFFICER. Hollins, George. 12th Battalion Green Howards. Says here: 'A cheery and sober chap.'

GEORGE. Yes, sir. Thank you, sir.

OFFICER. Conditions, injuries, diseases?

GEORGE. Puncture wound. Right foot.

OFFICER. All healed, now?

GEORGE. Yes, sir.

OFFICER. Good man. Now, are we giving you civvies or do you want to buy your own?

GEORGE (*confused*). Umm…

OFFICER. Chop chop, Private, you're one of millions!

GEORGE. My own. Sir.

OFFICER. Got your fifty-three shillings?

GEORGE *pats his pocket.*

GEORGE. Sir.

OFFICER. Dispersal certificate?

GEORGE. Sir.

OFFICER. Unfathomable feeling of dread?

*Beat.*

GEORGE (*taken aback*). Sir?

*Pause. The* OFFICER *and* GEORGE *lock eyes. The* OFFICER *has a small piece of paper.*

OFFICER. One train ticket to – (*Studies the ticket.*) Scarborough. Home, Hollins.

GEORGE *takes it. Looks at it.*

GEORGE (*to himself*). Home. I'm going home. I'm going home I'm going

*Switch to* FRANKIE *and three of his army section.*

ARMY BUDDY ONE. Home, you fucking prick!

ARMY BUDDY THREE. Nice bit of R and R! /

ARMY BUDDY TWO. Soft duvets, real pillows –

ARMY BUDDY THREE. Proper fucking milk from a cow's tit!

FRANKIE. Yeah, I just wish it wasn't / like –

ARMY BUDDY TWO. Oh kebabs! *Nando's*, Frank!

ARMY BUDDY THREE. You'll bring us back some Peri Peri, yeah?

FRANKIE. Lads, I don't think I'm gonna / be coming back

ARMY BUDDY TWO. And what the fuck do you know? Prick.

ARMY BUDDY ONE. WOMEN Frankie! Fucking women! /

FRANKIE. Yeah…

ARMY BUDDY ONE. And your mam.

ARMY BUDDY THREE. She's a woman.

ARMY BUDDY ONE. Look at him! Getting all hard thinking about your mam!

ARMY BUDDY THREE. Shut up!

ARMY BUDDY TWO. You're a lucky fucking duck at the end of the day, kid, / really.

FRANKIE (*snaps*). You'd trade with me then, would ya? Any of ya?

*Beat. Slightly awkward.*

ARMY BUDDY ONE. It'll blow over, Frank. You'll see.

FRANKIE. And there's punches in the arm and kisses on the head
And knees in the knackers
Then me and Sarge speed away
till their faces are tiny

then pinpricks
then nothing.
I look out the window
count the
rocks

CHORUS. And

FRANKIE. Mountains

CHORUS. And

FRANKIE. Compounds

CHORUS. And

*Switch to* GEORGE.

GEORGE. Blackened trees

CHORUS. And

GEORGE. Scorched earth

CHORUS. And

GEORGE. Shell holes
Of Passchendaele
The hellhole
The mudhole
Where we lost them…
Whoosh past the window
And it's gone.

*Switch to* NAT, *who is swiping through his tablet.* ELIAS *sleeps heavily next to him.* NAT *speaks in a whisper.*

CHORUS. And

NAT. ID card

CHORUS. And

NAT. Travel doc

CHORUS. And

NAT. Contact address. YES!

NAT *kisses the tablet, puts it in his bag.*

CHORUS. Checked. Packed. Zipped.
It's dawn.
The worn canvas of the tarpaulin glistens with dew
Early summer sun creeps through cracks in the chipboard walls.

ELIAS *stirs.* NAT *quickly sits on his bag.* ELIAS *has hair in his face, yawns.*

ELIAS. What time is it?

NAT. Just after six.

ELIAS. Did you have the dream again?

NAT. No.

ELIAS. Then you've been up all night on that thing? (*Points to tablet.*) I've told you, there's nothing you / can do for –

NAT. You said you'd go to the kitchens for scraps.

ELIAS *groans.*

Elias! All the good shit will be gone by seven.

ELIAS *rolls out of bed, shakes his head. Stretches. Grabs his shoes – starts to head out, ruffling* NAT*'s hair roughly as he does.*

ELIAS. Okay. See you at the generator.

NAT. Cool.

ELIAS *laughs and shakes his head.*

ELIAS. 'Cool'.

ELIAS *slopes off.* NAT *pauses. He goes to where* ELIAS *was lying. Feels under the makeshift bed, finds a few screwed-up notes, a lighter and a large pouch of tobacco. He looks to the door, looks at his finds, thinks, then shoves them back under. He puts on his bag.*

CHORUS. Nat has one last look around
His makeshift shack
And out on to this tented town

NAT. This city has chewed me up and spat me out

FRANKIE. This landscape has swallowed me whole

GEORGE. This country has split me in two.
And my shadow will stay here
Fighting a war till the end of

*Switch to* FRANKIE.

CHORUS. Time passes.
The airbase, a lofty airport hangar;
Frankie lurks in a corner
toking on a fag.
His cough echoes through the rafters
Where a black-tailed bird is trying to escape
Circling and squawking and flapping its wings.

*Switch to* GEORGE.

GEORGE. The light is dim
Every man around me sleeps
But the lashing rain
And the train's throb and rattle
Keep me awake.

NAT. I take a short-cut through the east camp
'Little England'
(I dream of hedgerows
Of neat white terraced houses)
I dart in between tents and
Shipping containers
Leap mounds of shoes and
Baby clothes and
Burning rubbish and

GEORGE. I study my reflection in the black outside
I close my eyes, listen to their breathing;
When I was a boy I used to creep on to the landing

And crouch outside my parents' door
And listen for their breaths.
When I was a boy
When I was a boy I –

*Overwhelmed by the thought of his childhood, his voice breaks.*

*Switch to* NAT *– breathless.*

NAT. Wait. What's that?
Tinny music playing
From a shit phone
A sound from my childhood:
My home
Rihanna or Beyoncé?
Stops me in my tracks
Takes me back
I'm outside the VRcade
with my brother
Our brains buzzing with anticipation
Ready to be filled with colour and sound

*He opens his palms as though soaking up the memory.*
ELIAS *appears – or is heard – in the distance, with a bag of spoils.*

ELIAS. Nat!

NAT. I pretend I don't hear him.

ELIAS. I've got Haugpølse!
I've got bread rolls and fish spread – Look!
Where are you going? Hey!

NAT. I turn away.

ELIAS. Where are you going with all your stuff?

NAT. And I run.
The smell of shit and burning plastic in my nose
Sweat and rainwater soaking through my clothes
Run run run
Like a kid tearing through back-of-his-hand streets

For no reason but to feel the earth under his feet
His body in motion
Knowing I won't see him again.
Elias.
Head down, temporary nest flown.
One word repeated in my head

NAT *and* CHORUS. HOME.

*Switch to* GEORGE.

CHORUS. In sight.
George pressed tight against the ship's rail
The decks and rigging team with men
Straining, craning to get a look
At the white chalk cliffs of their dreams

*Switch to* FRANKIE.

Frankie feels weak
Tugs on the peak of his baseball cap – slumps down in
his seat
What's worse, he thinks
A plane full of fat suntanned Brits?
Or the Army TriStar they flew to Cyprus?
The air thick with bitterness; silent.
He looks down. Nothing but vast blue seas and

*Switch to* NAT *with* TRAFFICKER *and* KIM. (*English translation in bold, which should be subtitled*). *They are sitting in a shipping container playing chess or cards.* NAT *stands away from – awkward.*

NAT. Please.

TRAFFICKER. Norsk. (**Norwegian.**) Snakker du ikke Norsk? (**Don't you speak?**)

NAT. Bare litt. (**Only a little.**) You don't speak English?

TRAFFICKER. Selvfølgelig gjør jeg det din tulling. Men du er i Norge. (**Of course I do, you fool. But you are in Norway.**)

KIM. Jævla engelske rotte. (**Fucking English rat!**)

NAT. Engelske! Ja! Engelske??

*They laugh a bit.*

TRAFFICKER. Okay okay. Speak.

*They stop playing for a while and give him their attention.*

NAT. I want to go to England. North-east region.

*They are shocked and slightly amused.*

TRAFFICKER. North-east? You're crazy?

NAT. It's back in government control now, there's a truce.

TRAFFICKER. You think a truce means peace? You're dreaming.

NAT. I'll risk it.

TRAFFICKER. Crazy crazy. Where did you get my details?

NAT. From Lars at the north camp kitchen.

TRAFFICKER *nods – sizing* NAT *up.*

TRAFFICKER. Stavanger to Newcastle… one hundred thousand krone.

NAT. That's four times what I paid to get here!

TRAFFICKER. Inflation, my friend.

NAT *sighs.*

NAT. I've got the money.

NAT *starts fiddling with his tablet.*

TRAFFICKER. You feel you're not welcome here. I understand. My government wants to say goodbye to you. You use up our resources. You take over our cities with your dirty ways. Drinking on the street and shitting in the gutter.

NAT. Yep. (*Tablet powers up.*)

TRAFFICKER. But what do you think you'll find in England? Work? Food? Hope? There's no hope. And there's no coming back, can't apply for refuge twice.

NAT (*still fiddling with the tablet*). I know.

*The* TRAFFICKER *touches the tablet, stopping* NAT *fiddling, lowering it so he can look into* NAT*'s eyes.*

TRAFFICKER. Then why leave?

NAT. Look, can you take me or not?

NAT *holds out the tablet. Points out a figure – proof he has the money.*

TRAFFICKER. Okay okay.

TRAFFICKER *takes it. Taps in a web address, some details.* NAT *looks at* KIM, *smiles nervously,* KIM *grunts.*

You make payment to this account. You use this reference and your handle. Okay? Message will tell you an address in Sola. You wait here, this address. Don't go anywhere for walk or snacks because you will miss your chance. Tomorrow. Maybe Monday. 2.30 a.m. We always go at 2.30 a.m. (*Gestures to* KIM.) This is Kim. He will get you. Kim is a professional. Don't fuck with Kim.

KIM. Don't fuck.

NAT. O… kay… Takk. (**Thank you.**)

TRAFFICKER. But there is risk. Always risk. Of death.

NAT. I understand.

TRAFFICKER. Only God can guide your way.

KIM *stands.*

KIM. Spør ham om han har sett landet sitt nylig? (*No subtitle.*)

NAT. What did he say?

TRAFFICKER. He says have you seen your country recently?

**Arriving**

*Switch to* GEORGE.

GEORGE. My country.
My country!
We've swung into the harbour
And we've taken to the streets.
Neat lines of war-beaten men
There's crowds and bands and flags and songs.
See the conquering hero comes
Sound the trumpets! Beat the drums!

*Switch to* FRANKIE. *He wakes with a start.*

FRANKIE. Fuck.

CHORUS. Seatbelts on and luggage stowed
And Frankie's dread begins to grow.

*Switch to* GEORGE.

GEORGE. Men break away
Tear into the crowd
The sun appears from behind a cloud
And I stop
Look up
The winter sun on my face
This is England.
And I breathe.

FRANKIE. Conveyer belts and
Hungover teenagers
Sunburnt pensioners and
Screaming kids
This is England

GEORGE. I taste salt.

FRANKIE. I can't breathe.

GEORGE. Tears?
No, George.

I won't cry.
For the boys. Or the sea. Or for Rosie. Or for me.
Home to Scarborough
I grasp my bag tight, scan the sea of faces
Not her.
Not her.
There are butterflies in my chest.
There are madly flapping birds in my chest
I think I might
Take flight

FRANKIE. One foot

GEORGE. I get swallowed

FRANKIE. In front of the other

GEORGE. A sea of people

FRANKIE. I follow the signs

GEORGE. I follow the crowd

FRANKIE. And just keep moving

GEORGE. Forward. We keep moving forward because we don't know how to

FRANKIE. Stop. At the arrival hall. Who will be here to meet me? My sister Kayleigh, like always?

GEORGE. Is she there?

FRANKIE. No.

GEORGE. There she is!

FRANKIE. She's not there.

GEORGE. My girl.

*Beat.*

FRANKIE. But there's a man in a creased shirt and dark glasses holding a scrawled sign:
*Frank Musgrave.*

GEORGE. She looks… different.
*Smaller*. Than I remember.
Her lips are redder and
She's *smoking*.
I've never seen her smoke before!
I don't know if I
Like it
She's *looking* for me
And
And
For a moment I want to run
(*Maybe begins to back away.*)
WHO AM I?

ROSE. George!

GEORGE. And everything stops.

*They embrace.*

**Crossing**

*Switch to* NAT *in a small motorboat on the sea with* KIM *and* ALDO, *another man making the trip from Norway to England. The sea is a little rough. The motor stops – reacting to a flashing light.*

NAT. Why have we stopped?

KIM. Shhhh.

ALDO (*under his breath*). Relax.

NAT. Oh God.

*They wait with bated breath. The light passes.*

ALDO. Alt Klart. **(All clear.)**

KIM *revs the engine up again.* ALDO *speaks to* NAT.

Okay?

NAT (*lying*). Fine.

ALDO *passes him a water bottle.*

Thanks.

NAT *takes a drink. Coughs it out.* KIM *and* ALDO *laugh.*

Jesus. Akevitt?

ALDO *takes it back.*

ALDO. Of course! You thought it was water? Skål.

ALDO *drinks.* NAT *looks around him in a panic.*

Relax. On the way back this boat will be *full*. That's when you have to worry.

NAT. I know. I did it three years ago. We had… thirty people in a boat this size?

ALDO. Thirty? Kim will fit sixty. People still streaming, from the north-east most.

NAT. Sixty? That's fucking / disgusting

KIM (*barks*). Hva? **(What?)**

NAT *checks himself – don't fuck with* KIM.

NAT. Nothing.

*A big wave.*

Jesus Christ! Sorry, I'm… nervous. When I travelled to Norway the engine failed. We capsized twelve miles off Egersund, a steamer picked us up.

ALDO. It happens. Did they get all of you?

NAT. No.

ALDO. Lose anyone?

NAT (*shaking his head*). I was travelling alone.

ALDO. Not many going back. You've got family in England?

NAT *doesn't say anything.*

Without people it's just bricks and rocks, my friend. You know the Norwegian Government would have deported you for free?

NAT. I can't cross the border. Can't go through the checkpoints.

ALDO. So you're a rebel?

*Beat.*

NAT. No.

ALDO. Then you dodged your draft? Your 'national service'? Didn't want to fight for your country?

NAT. I can't kill. For anyone. Government or rebels.

ALDO. You know they'll arrest you as soon as they see you!

NAT. I have to find my brother.

ALDO. You left him in England?

NAT *is defensive.*

NAT. We got separated!

ALDO *nods,* NAT *thinks he is unconvinced.*

I was going to send for him. Get work in the factories, send money home for his transport. Maybe even study in Bergen: a new life for us. We hear so much about Norway! Amazing healthcare, great quality of life… /

ALDO. Yes yes. But these are false dreams.

NAT. I know. I never even made it past the camps in Grønland. Took nine months to get out of the holding unit! Since then they've been 'processing my application'.

ALDO (*joining in*). 'Processing your application'?

NAT *nods and looks down.* ALDO *leans forward.*

It's a shithouse, isn't it?

NAT. What?

ALDO. Life.

*ALDO reaches out his hand. NAT begins to warm to him.*

Aldo.

NAT. Nat.

*He gives NAT another drink.*

What's in the bags?

ALDO. Insulin and penicillin. Whisky and cigarettes… other essentials.

NAT. Whisky and cigarettes – essentials?

*He laughs a bit.*

ALDO. The *most* essential! When did you last speak to him?

NAT. It's been – two years. We lost touch when he joined the rebels.

ALDO. Which faction?

NAT. North Sea Alliance.

ALDO. Ruthless.

NAT. But I've been following him online – on the freedom forums and his timelines so I can check he's okay. Everything stops seven weeks ago.

ALDO. Where's home?

NAT. Scarborough.

ALDO. Oh fuck.

NAT. Yep. Riots. Protests. Dead on the streets.

ALDO. Worse than that.

NAT. Worse?

ALDO. What's The Spa?

NAT. What?

ALDO. Scarborough Spa, what is it?

NAT. It's like this grand old hall where they have concerts and shows and stuff. Why?

ALDO. Our friend Rolf told us: the rebels were using it as a base since the end of last year. The army stormed it. By ground and air. Fucking bloodbath.

NAT. When was this?

ALDO. Kim?

KIM. Syv uker siden.

*Beat.*

ALDO. About seven weeks ago.

*Pause.*

NAT. I still need to try and find him.

ALDO. And if you can't?

NAT. I want to walk along the North Bay. I want to see the sea.

KIM. Sjøen er der enda.

NAT. What?

ALDO. He says the sea is still there!

NAT. Right. Good.

*They laugh a bit,* KIM *softening for the first time. It fades.*

ALDO. You need to stay off the main roads, my friend. Check points every few miles. You'll have to cross the Moors.

NAT. Fuck that! I'll get lost!

ALDO. You won't. You'll see. You've got the weather on your side. The 'British Summertime'.

ALDO *looks at him.*

I'll help you, Nat.

NAT. Thank you.

*The engine stops.* NAT *panics a bit.*

What's happening?

ALDO. Shhh.

NAT. Why have we stopped? Is it the engine?

ALDO. Relax. This is just something we like to do, me and Kim.

*Beat. Both* KIM *and the* ALDO *have closed their eyes.*

What can you hear?

NAT. Nothing. The waves.

ALDO. Exactly.

KIM. Verden er full av skriking og blod. Vil du aldri kun ha litt fred? **(The world is full of shouting and blood. Don't you ever just want some peace?)**

**Celebrations**

*Switch to* GEORGE.

CHORUS. George wants some peace.
A celebratory drink at the pub
Overloads his senses.

GEORGE. Faces, once familiar, loom like gargoyles
Everyone wants a piece of me, to toast me
I smile and nod and join in the singing
I laugh at jokes without hearing the punchline

CHORUS. But inside he folds in on himself
Flesh tightens around his bones
He closes his eyes for a moment and

GEORGE. The crash of the surf
A cold-salt-air slap in the face
The wind braces
The world spins on its axis
But there she is, my girl
Writing 'I-Love-You's in the sand
Petticoats trailing in the wash
Staggering, spinning, laughing
Raising her arms wide as though
She's trying to
Hold the sky
She's frightening me
I blink again and

ROSE *and* GEORGE *have a bottle of beer each.* GEORGE *is nervous, he doesn't know why.*

ROSE. To England. To Scarborough. To my boy.

GEORGE *clinks bottles with her and drinks. Looks around.*

GEORGE. Have you… moved things around?

ROSE. No. It's the same as it was last time you had leave.

GEORGE. Right.

ROSE. George!

*Beat. She runs out of the door. Runs back in. Stops in the doorway.* GEORGE *is irritated.*

GEORGE. What are you doing?

ROSE. I just wanted to know what it feels like to walk into a room and for you to be there. I'd forgotten. It's wonderful.

GEORGE. Don't be silly, Rosie.

ROSE. How proud you must have felt tonight. How proud I felt on your arm! To be a *hero*, George!

GEORGE. Come and sit.

ROSE. Come and *dance*!

GEORGE. You're drunk! /

ROSE. I know! And I'm delirious! /

GEORGE. We don't have any music.

*She grabs his hand – pulls him up.*

ROSE. I'll hum!

*She pulls him close. She begins humming and they do a simple waltz. He is reluctant at first but then becomes transfixed by her. This is what he's been waiting for – this intimacy – he basks in it, nestling his face in her neck. They dance. Then, as they turn,* ROSE *becomes a dead soldier* (TIBBS), *lifeless and heavy and hard for* GEORGE *to support. As they complete a full turn she is* ROSE *again.*

GEORGE *steps away – spooked. He becomes fidgety.*

What's the matter?

*He is jumpy – intense suddenly as though something has changed. He speaks with urgency – the need to get something out.*

GEORGE. Do you remember my section, Rose?

ROSE. You mean the Green How/ards?

GEORGE. No that's the *battalion* that's bigger than a section. I told you about them. In my letters I used to…

ROSE. Remind me.

*He delivers at a pace.*

GEORGE. Robbie Hebdon. Terrible eczema. Lied about his age and joined at fifteen.

ROSE. That's far too young / to

GEORGE. Arnold Potter. Pots. He could do magic, Rose, real close-up sleight-of hand-magic. Percy Strickland was simple – but he had a good heart. Will Barker had a beautiful voice but terrible feet, smelt like the latrines.

ROSE *laughs.*

Les Booth used to cry for his mother in his sleep but we never told him.

ROSE. You poor / things

GEORGE. Greg Bowes had a baby girl, Ida. Six months old when we left for Boulogne. That could have been us, if you'd had your way.

ROSE. Well, now I'm glad we waited / for

GEORGE. Cecil Moss had pimples. Henry was angry. Albert was shy. Eric Sharp was just that! Sharp as a tack. I used to like to be on patrol with Eric.

And Ronald Tibbs.

ROSE. Oh, of course, / Tibbsy!

GEORGE. The joker. He was the bloody best of the lot.

ROSE. I'd like to meet them, George.

GEORGE. Enough. Stop it now.

GEORGE *sits with his head in his hands.* ROSE *crouches in front of him, confused.*

ROSE (*softly*). George?

GEORGE *looks up, then, as if coming round.*

GEORGE. I'm fine. Sorry, Rosie. I think… I just wanted to say their names out loud. Don't know why.

ROSE. I love you.

GEORGE. I love you.

*Beat.*

Do we have any Scotch?

**Taxi**

CHORUS. Worn grey fabric under Frankie's fingers
No aircon and the sickly smell of Magic Tree.
The taxi driver chatters into his hands-free
It's a language Frankie recognises.
Pashto.
To have that language *here*:
Dangerous, familiar yet unknown
Makes his worlds crash into one another.
WHAT IS HOME? He thinks.
And where?

*A note is stuck to* FRANKIE*'s front door.*

FRANKIE. 'Migraine. Let me sleep it off. Ham in fridge. M.'

When did Mum become 'M'?

I stand in the middle of the lounge and drop my bag.
And this is usually where it starts: The Big Unwind.
In seconds, can in my hand.
Phone blowing up with texted plans.
The Lion: Luke, and Ket and Ryan.
And Mum saying 'Not those dickheads, Frank – they'll drag you down.'
But how could I come back to town and not see
The Original Cross Street Crew?
Ket grew to be like family when we were kids.
What with his mum always off her tits
Anyway: Feet up. Tea and biscuits.
Mum and Kayleigh. Little Jenson
Jumping all over his Uncle Frankie
Asking to see his gun
And Nan.
Her very own Scarborough war hero
Will take her for scones and tea at The Spa
And we'll listen to the band, and the waves…

I perch on the edge of the couch.
Not ready to slop or slouch yet
Look at the set of frames on the side

Mum in her twenties, Kayleigh at five
Me – the cutest Cub Scout in the world
Doing photobombs before they were even a thing
I close my eyes
Try to jump back to those times;
Summer 6 p.m. but the pavement slabs are still hot.
And we've got shepherd's pie for tea
We've played all day
Power Rangers
Teenage Mutant Ninja Turtles
And soldiers
Shooting the shit
out of each other
For kicks.

But the clock ticks.
Fridge hums.
And the kitchen
smells of smoke and bleach.
I stare out of the glass at the oak tree
In the garden
That's as old as me

**The Hat**

*Switch to* GEORGE *and* ROSE. *Later – they sit at either end of the bed – drinking whisky.*

GEORGE. You're staring. Rose?

ROSE. What are you thinking about?

GEORGE. Nothing.

ROSE. I was thinking about that little B&B in Whitby. With the Border Collies. We drank whisky in bed then, do you remember?

GEORGE. Yes.

ROSE. And we didn't know war had broken out. There were crowds in the street! And we just lay in bed drinking, listening to the rain. Married a week. The whole world was opening up like a great big oyster. The war didn't feel like anything to do with us, did it?

GEORGE. No.

ROSE. We can put this behind us now. Shall we go to bed?

*Pause. She clearly means for more than sleep. He is shocked by how uncomfortable this makes him.*

GEORGE. Not… yet.

ROSE. Well, let's get you out of these clothes. Into something cosy.

*She goes to start to unbutton his shirt. He pulls away.*

GEORGE. You don't need to.

*He takes another big swig.* ROSE *is perturbed.*

ROSE. Let's get you unpacked then.

GEORGE. It can wait!

ROSE. It stinks of boys.

*He watches her begin to unpack – it feels like a profound invasion of privacy. He feels so frustrated and he's not sure why. Then –*

Oh my goodness!

GEORGE. What?

ROSE. George, close your eyes.

GEORGE. No more games!

ROSE. Close them!

*He does reluctantly. She holds a dishevelled German soldier's hat and looks at it with morbid fascination. She puts it on her head.*

Alright now… Open!

*He does.*

GEORGE *tenses up*. ROSE *is excited. She looks at herself in the mirror.*

GEORGE. Rose – take it off /

ROSE. Is this from a Jerry you killed? Is it?

GEORGE. Have some respect!

ROSE. Respect – for the *Germans*???

GEORGE. Respect for life.

ROSE (*incredulous*). For the baby-killers of Scarborough? Four years ago we woke up to Jerry warships bursting through the fog! We ran through the streets, in our nightclothes, your mother hysterical and freezing. They shelled babes in prams and Boy Scouts.

GEORGE. Of course I remember. You don't understand /

ROSE. And do you remember our walk along the front the next day? With the turrets and flags from the Arcadia twisted and broken on the path in front.

GEORGE. You don't need to tell me, it's why I enlisted, / Rose!

ROSE. I hope you did shoot him – right in the chest! /

GEORGE (*loud*). TAKE IT OFF!

GEORGE *lunges towards her – making a grab for the hat. She cowers, he grabs it. He holds it, transfixed. Turns to the audience.*

Shall I tell her?

Shall I tell her how on Christmas Eve we waited with bated breath, wondering if it could happen again? And how, sure enough, the guns go quiet at midnight and we hear the most *beautiful* singing? In German. And they shout to us to sing too. So we belt out some crummy carol, and we are *terrible*! But we sing it anyway, and we burn braziers at the second parapet and the Germans send up star shells that light up the sky over No Man's Land. Like fireworks.

Would she believe that despite orders that 'there is to be NO repeat of last year's fraternisation' at dawn we make our way through to the front. And we shake hands with them. We swap names, gifts: buttons for brandy, cigarettes for jam. We drink. We laugh. We talk in broken German and English. No Man's Land becomes Every Man's Land.

Shall I tell her that we are able to bury our dead, some of our lads who've been lying there for weeks rotting into the earth? Would she believe me if I told her that the Germans help us pick them up, gently, and bring them to the graves we dig? And we do the same for them.

Shall I tell Rose that when we get back to our dugout there's a Jerry in it, drunk and singing! *In* our dugout! He's got a bottle of Scotch and he staggers towards me, puts his hat on my head and his bottle to my lips. 'Trink! Trink!' he says. We know we've got to get him out before the Sarge gets back so Tibbs and I grab him, one under each arm, and deliver him back to their line laughing all the way, like three old chums. Shall I tell her that we get back to the dugout I find this. (*Holds that hat.*) 'That will be a nice Christmas souvenir.' I think.

Could I tell her that later, when Sarge is back and we're settling down to our extra rations, we hear 'Freund! Neuer freund!' And it's that damn Fritz again! Staggering towards our trench still drunk as a skunk.

And Sarge gives me the order.

Fritz sees me. Grins. Opens his arms

It's quick. In the chest. And he falls.

I cry after. Like a boy.

Do I tell her?

No. I just say:

(*To* ROSE.) Yes. I was following orders. I follow orders.

**Mum**

MUM *appears in the doorway in a dressing gown. She looks at* FRANKIE *for a long time.*

MUM. Son.

FRANKIE *turns. They look at each other.*

FRANKIE. Why haven't you answered any of my messages?

MUM (*pointedly*). We've been busy.

FRANKIE. Too busy to speak to me?

MUM. Your sister's in a state. Your nan's had a urine infection and this phone hasn't stopped ringing.

FRANKIE. Who's ringing?

MUM. Who do you reckon? Newspapers. Reporters. Prank-callers. Should have gone ex-directory years ago.

FRANKIE. Reporters? About me?

MUM. Well, they're certainly not interested in me.

FRANKIE. What have they been saying?

MUM. You're lucky they've even let you back here. When's your thingy?

FRANKIE. What thingy?

MUM (*quietly*). Court case. When's that start?

FRANKIE. Dunno. Soon. I've been back for hours, Mum.

MUM. Well, what did you expect, Frankie? Balloons? Banners?

FRANKIE (*getting riled*). A fucking HUG maybe!

MUM. Oi! You're not on tour now!

*These sharp words put* FRANKIE *in his place.*

FRANKIE. Sorry. Is Nan alright?

*Beat.*

Mum? Will she be alright?

MUM. Course she will. She'll outlive us all. Kayleigh's with her.

*A lighter moment between them. A sense of relief.*

FRANKIE. Can I go round?

MUM. She's not up to visitors.

FRANKIE. Kayleigh's there!

MUM. Yeah – well, she's a girl.

FRANKIE. So?

MUM. It's a urine infection, isn't it? It's a woman's thing

FRANKIE (*getting angry*). BOLLOCKS! 'Woman's thing'!

MUM. I don't know what to tell you, Frank!

FRANKIE. So Nan knows. It's been in the paper?

*She says nothing.*

Mum, I was in solitary at Bastion right up till I left.

MUM. What, and you haven't checked your phone?

FRANKIE *shakes his head.*

FRANKIE. Switched it off. I swear. What have they been saying, Mum?

MUM (*her voice breaks*). Monster.

*This shakes* FRANKIE.

FRANKIE. Yeah?

MUM. 'Sick soldier's spree of violence.'

FRANKIE. What in the *Gazette*?

MUM. The *Gazette*? That's *The* fucking *Sun*, Frankie!

*Utter shock.*

FRANKIE. What?

MUM. This morning.

FRANKIE. Can I see it?

MUM. Oh yeah, I'll just go and get me scrapbook, shall I? I saw it in Budgens.

*Beat.* FRANKIE*'s world is imploding.*

FRANKIE. Has Nan seen it?

MUM. She gets it delivered! I couldn't get down the newsagent quick enough.

FRANKIE. Oh God. Mum? You haven't seen the…

*Beat.*

MUM. Video?

*The word is utterly loaded.*

FRANKIE. Yeah.

*She says nothing. For a long time.*

*I* haven't seen it. Is it really…?

*The unfinished question hangs in the air.*

MUM. It's not my son. (*Beat.*) It's not my son on that video, no.

FRANKIE. I'm your son.

MUM. I was so proud of how you turned yourself around. But you're worse than that thug Ryan.

*He moves towards her a little and she backs away.*

No. /

FRANKIE. I'm your son, Mum. It's still me, still Golden Balls.

MUM. Don't TOUCH ME!

FRANKIE (*advancing*). I'd never hurt you!

*Beat. He is shaken. She softens.*

MUM. Look, why don't you take your bag upstairs? Have a bath. I've left towels on your bed.

FRANKIE. Yeah, yeah…

*He grabs his bag. Moves towards the door. He's embarrassed but asks anyway.*

Will you come up?

MUM. What?

FRANKIE. Will you come up?

MUM. And do what?

FRANKIE. I dunno. Sit on the end of the bed. Smoke a fag. Play Angry Birds on your phone, I don't know. Just –

Be there.

*Beat.*

MUM. Go have a sleep, Frankie.

*Switch to all three in focus.*

FRANKIE (*not to* MUM). Sleep?

## ACT TWO

### A Foot on English Soil

NAT. They drop me at a deserted harbour a few miles from the Port of Tyne – where we check for connection. Aldo tells me to drop a pin here and send it to this contact. I watch them go.
And wait.
For my heart to explode.

I have set foot on the soil of my kin
I have come home. England, let me in!

*An incoming alert on* NAT*'s tablet.*

'Walk through ferry tunnel NW and wait at other end.'

NAT *looks around for the tunnel.*

NAT *enters the tunnel.*

The air is hot and stale, nothing but the sound of my feet
And my heartbeat. Feels like I'm walking into the guts of a city
Into the dark heart of some forgotten land
Can't see my hand in front of my face.

NAT *uses his tablet as a light.*

My walk
Becomes a jog
Becomes a race

And as the tunnel twists and turns
No light
Feels like
it might
go on forever
And

Adrenalin takes over
Fear flickers in the vein in my temple
Arteries pump pure panic
Acid blood
Acrid sweat
Another turn another bend then
Light
Life
End.

*He stops running. Breathing heavily – hands on his knees.* NAT *sits.*

*He uses his tablet to beam some videos on the curved wall of the tunnel. He and his brother playing when they were kids – walking along the coast at Scarborough with their mum, possibly? Then his brother* FINN, *alone, playing up to the camera.* NAT *reaches out his hand as though he could touch the screen but it suddenly changes to a picture of* ELIAS *and 'VIDEO CALL FROM ELIAS' flashes up. Then, from behind him, a voice barks: 'Hey!'*

NAT *jumps up and puts both hands up, in the direction of the noise, the projection beaming onto his face.*

Four of us, squeezed in the back of a tiny car. The driver smokes cigarettes and keeps the windows closed. Every now and again:

CHORUS. GET DOWN.

*All four in the back of the car duck.*

Okay.

*They sit up again.*

NAT. Transfer. A lorry. Smells of meat and sawdust. Flashlights, whispers. Scrabbling in the dark. The shipping container; we meet again. Time for one deep breath and then

Hatch locked.

*Dark.* NAT *powers up his tablet and finds he is not alone. He jumps. There is another man* (REBEL) *in there, the tablet lights his face. He looks morose.* NAT *clocks the way he is dressed.*

Hello.

*The* REBEL *says nothing.* NAT *sees his opportunity to try to get information.*

Where are you coming from?

*Beat. No response.*

Are you going home? To find family?

*The* REBEL *looks at him – says nothing.*

You're… North Sea Alliance. Right?

*The* REBEL *tenses.* NAT *reaches into his bag.*

It's okay. My brother is with the Alliance.

*He brings out a bottle of whisky he got from* ALDO. *Holds it out.*

You might know him?

*The* REBEL *takes it.* NAT *shows him a video on his tablet.*

Finn. He was thirteen here. He would be sixteen now. Joined at fourteen.

REBEL. And you?

*Beat.*

NAT. I've been in Norway. Grønland camp.

REBEL. You left him?

NAT. No! We got separated! When we left. We were promised seats and lifejackets; we had neither. We had our place on the boat, then this woman on the banks blew her whistle – she had lifejackets for minors. I told him to get one, he stood a much better chance then. I kept our place on the boat, I watched him every second while he waded to shore. He was standing in line, looking at me. They started the motor. I tried to get off. I tried to get to him. They wouldn't stop.

*The* REBEL *looks unconvinced.*

REBEL. I don't know Finn.

*The* REBEL *leans up against the shipping container wall, preparing to get some sleep.*

NAT. One more thing. The assault on The Spa in Scarborough. The Alliance were using it as a base?

*The* REBEL *nods towards* NAT*'s bag.* NAT *sighs, takes out a packet of cigarettes he got from* ALDO *– hands them over.*

REBEL. What about it?

NAT. Were there… survivors?

REBEL. None.

*Beat.*

NAT. You're sure?

REBEL. It was a bloodbath. The last push. Except…

NAT. Go on?

REBEL. They took a group of hostages.

NAT. Yes??

*The* REBEL *pauses.* NAT *sighs, reaches in his bag – some pouches of rice – offers them. The* REBEL *takes them.*

REBEL. Slaughtered.

NAT. You're sure?

REBEL. They would have been tortured for information. None of them would have betrayed the Alliance! If your brother was one of them – you should be proud.

NAT (*sadly*). Right.

*The* REBEL *feels a pang of pity.*

REBEL. Let me see him again.

*Beat.* NAT *beams* FINN *onto the wall of the shipping container. They both watch him for a while.*

I don't know him.

**The First Night**

CHORUS. Sleep is no place for George now.

NAT. Sleep calls as I stare at the star-studded sky.

FRANKIE. Sleep is nowhere as I stare at the white Artex ceiling.

GEORGE. Never

FRANKIE. Follow the stars

GEORGE. Again

NAT. Track the constellations.

FRANKIE. The stick'n'glo stars me and Kayleigh saved up for

NAT. The Plough and Polaris

FRANKIE. The world map of damp!

GEORGE. Nothing. Ever –

CHORUS. George doesn't dare close his eyes, afraid of sleep afraid of

FRANKIE. Dreams. Of escape. Discovering new countries. Dreams are made in towns like these and

NAT. I'm dropped at a deserted station. The railway that cuts across the Moors is my guide, though the trains haven't run since before I left. A bottle of water, bag of snacks, I'm following the tracks. Along the way the litter and debris of thousands who have left searching for a new life. But they left and I return. I yearn for home as I veer forward – my fear draining from me because –

This is the sky of my dreams. However bleak it seems, I *feel* him. I feel his heart beating in this same land and

GEORGE. Nothing will ever –

FRANKIE. Me and Nan spotting boats from my window:
*A tiny boat floats out on the sea:*
*Where are you going? Can you take me?*

GEORGE. Ever – will be –

NAT. There's a kindness to the sky.
And a wildness; England!

CHORUS. George sits on the edge of the bed and looks out on to the Bay.

FRANKIE. I curl up in a ball, try to make myself small again

NAT. I lie in a star shape, feel the earth underneath me

CHORUS. Rose sleeps beside him like a china doll
And he feels a fool
His brow is wet. His fists wound tight

GEORGE. Nothing – will – ever be alright

NAT (*looking around, quieter this time*). England.

GEORGE. Again.

FRANKIE. If walls could talk! All the wanks and the pukes and the fights and the fevers. The all-night Xbox sessions with Ket. The girls I sneaked up to my single bed.

NAT. I pull tufts of grass, rub the earth between my fingers! Bang my fists on the ground. I dig a shallow hole and scream into it.

FRANKIE. I listen to the waves that have washed me to sleep for twenty-four years. I drift.

NAT. I come to. Crawl into my tent, the weight of my grief on my back.

CHORUS. And as the rest of the world sleeps, George sits for hours, timing his breaths with the waves. Then comes the indefinite, unshapen dawn. And against the pink-orange sky – George makes out grey shadows. Irregular waves become lumpen forms, become tall. Become

GEORGE. Men.

CHORUS. Emerging from the water.

GEORGE. My men.

CHORUS. Larger than life. Washed out and grey.

GEORGE. Robbie and Potts. Eric and – and Tibbs.

CHORUS. Will they wave? Will they call? Are they really there at all?

GEORGE *watches intently.* FRANKIE *jumps up.*

FRANKIE. Days pass and I barricade myself.

NAT. Hours pass and I wake.

FRANKIE. Fags, instant noodles, squash and vodka.

NAT. And for a moment I'm back in Grønland – the camp with the dew dripping down from the tent.

FRANKIE. Curtains drawn. Door double-locked. Pace the lounge, chain smoking, screaming at Jeremy Kyle.

NAT. Outside the tent, birds sing.

FRANKIE. Outside the house, vermin reporters.

NAT. Fifteen missed calls from Elias.

FRANKIE. No Nan. No Jenson and Kayleigh's cold like a stranger.

Days pass.

NAT. Hours pass.

GEORGE. Weeks pass

CHORUS. And George folds further in on himself.

**Rose's Breaking Point 1**

ROSE *comes in, flustered. She doesn't say anything to* GEORGE. GEORGE *sits on the bed – still.*

GEORGE. Hello.

ROSE *takes her coat off.*

How are you?

ROSE. How am I? I slept frightfully. I was up at five. This is my fourth twelve-hour shift this week – the skin on my hands is cut to ribbons from the machines, I'm starving hungry, your mother has summoned to see me tonight and my head feels like it's a vice! How are you?

*Beat.*

GEORGE. Alright.

ROSE. Marvellous.

GEORGE. I'll make you something to eat.

ROSE. You'll only burn it.

*She strides into the kitchen. She makes an exasperated noise. She comes out holding piles of wet clothing.*

What's this?

GEORGE. I washed them.

ROSE. I can see that, but why didn't you put them through the mangle? (*Sniffs them.*) And how much soap did you use? They're not rinsed. Oh… George.

*She throws the clothes down in the sink.*

GEORGE. I'm sorry.

*She appears in the doorway, frustrated. Calms herself. Kinder:*

ROSE. This is so silly. You loping around here all day while *I'm* out working.

GEORGE. I've not been loping. I saw a cuckoo. That means spring's coming.

ROSE (*impatient*). When are you going to go back to work, George?

*This triggers a deep anxiety in* GEORGE. *He gets up.*

GEORGE. I'll rinse the clothes.

ROSE. Leave the clothes. You have to carry on /

GEORGE. IT'S TOO LOUD!

ROSE. It's a railway station, George, / of course it's loud!

GEORGE *falls to his knees, grabs* ROSE*'s skirt.*

GEORGE. Please don't make me go.

ROSE (*shocked*). George, get off your knees, you're not a CHILD!

*He sits on the bed again, head in hands. She sits next to him. Puts her hand in his. Talks soothingly.*

Mr Walker has been very kind to keep your job open as long as he has. It's time to get back to normal. You out at work and me at home with the… family.

GEORGE *gets up to leave the room.*

Where are you going?

GEORGE (*forgetting himself*). To the crapper.

ROSE. George!

GEORGE. I mean the WC.

*She stands in his way.*

ROSE. Don't run away. Look at me.

*He avoids her eye. Rubs his face. She moves his hand away from his face.*

Why do you keep doing that? You have to tell me what's wrong!

GEORGE. I'm fine. It's fine.

**Lifeline 1**

TONY *and* FRANKIE *are sitting on a bench on the seafront, holding polystyrene coffee cups.*

TONY. Glad you decided to come.

FRANKIE. You said you might be able to find me somewhere to stay?

TONY. Yeah. Finding housing can be a challenge for vets like you. (*Takes his phone out.*) Just turning this on flight mode, so we won't be disturbed.

*He puts his phone in his top pocket.*

FRANKIE. So, you're a charity?

TONY. Yeah, we're like Help for Heroes – but smaller. We do one-to-one stuff: counselling, support… Or just having coffee by the sea and chewing the fat.

FRANKIE. Didn't say much on your website.

TONY. Bane of my life that bloody website. We're going through a big 'tech revamp' at the moment, whatever that means. So it's sparse, yeah, sorry. What's the situation with where you're staying now?

*TONY gets his notebook out.*

FRANKIE. There's reporters there every day.

TONY. Wankers.

FRANKIE. My mum has to get out through the neighbour's house.

TONY. Well, that's a pain in the arse, Frankie… but /

FRANKIE. We've had threats.

TONY. What sort of threats?

FRANKIE. I don't really want to go into it.

TONY. I need some detail, mate. We've got this traffic-light-system thing. Green means mild need, amber means moderate, red means urgent. Need.

FRANKIE. Okay… we've had dogshit through the letter box. Someone smashed the front window. The front step doused with petrol. We've had graffiti. '*Racist army scum fuck off.*'

TONY. You weren't joking.

FRANKIE. If I go, they'll leave Mum alone. It's probably just kids!

TONY. Have you thought –

FRANKIE. What?

*Beat.*

TONY. I don't wanna panic you, Frankie, but what about the Islamic centre?

FRANKIE. No…

TONY. They could be targeting you. You're high-profile. You're basically a jihadi's wet dream.

FRANKIE. Fuck.

*Beat.*

TONY. Can I say something, off the record?

FRANKIE. How do you mean?

TONY. Well, I'm meant to be impartial; not express too much of an 'opinion'.

FRANKIE. Go on, what?

TONY. I am *fucking* livid for you, mate. Saying you've bought shame on your country. You're out there protecting your country! They don't know any of the stuff you've seen: the danger, the pain, the… loss.

FRANKIE *is intrigued by* TONY*'s insight.*

FRANKIE. Yeah?

TONY. My little brother died in Iraq. 4 Rifles – roadside bomb. I do this for him.

FRANKIE. I'm… sorry.

TONY. Yep. Four years since we lost Darren. But a vet doesn't have to *die* at war for us to lose them, do you get what I mean?

FRANKIE *nods. He feels understood for the first time.*

We don't want to lose you, Frankie.

FRANKIE. Thanks.

TONY. My brother would have done what you did.

FRANKIE *shifts uncomfortably.*

FRANKIE. Look, I just wanna find somewhere / to

TONY. You done any interviews yet?

FRANKIE. No way!

TONY. We can help with that.

FRANKIE. How?

TONY. We help veterans become media-savvy – if they're in touch with the press. Fucking gutter dogs, Frankie, our press. But you gotta do it.

FRANKIE. What's the point?

TONY. Tell people what it was like. A living hell, right? These people are ignorant. But you could turn it around.

FRANKIE. I dunno…

TONY *turns to him, intensely.*

TONY. Tell me now, like I'm one of those right-on-pacifist Twitter bastards.

FRANKIE. I can't.

TONY. Own it! It's your truth, Frank!

**Rose's Breaking Point 2**

*Runs on from last scene with* GEORGE *and* ROSE.

ROSE. I want the truth, George! Is it another girl?

GEORGE. What? No!

ROSE. You're gone half the night on your 'walks'.

GEORGE. I can't sleep.

ROSE. So you walk the streets?

GEORGE. Yes. Sometimes the beach. There's nobody but you; why would you say that?

ROSE. When we make love, you won't look at me.

GEORGE *is stunned.*

I thought maybe you'd been with one of those French whores.

GEORGE. NO! Of *course* I didn't. Leave me alone!

*He sits. He starts to rub his face again. She considers her next action. Then she barks orders at him, a bit like an army sergeant.*

ROSE. Come on, George. Come on – stand up, Georgie! That's it!

GEORGE *stands. A* DOCTOR *is examining him.* GEORGE *seems distant. Just grabbing onto the ends of sentences and the odd word. The* DOCTOR *circles him. The following is delivered at pace – almost overlapping.*

DOCTOR. Does he sweat?

ROSE. Does he sweat?

DOCTOR. Do you sweat, George?

ROSE. He trembles.

GEORGE. I do.

DOCTOR. He's not sleeping?

ROSE. No – he's not sleeping.

GEORGE. No sleep.

DOCTOR. At all?

ROSE. Hardly.

DOCTOR. George?

GEORGE. Hardly.

ROSE. He has nightmares.

DOCTOR (*holding his open palm up*). Punch my hand?

GEORGE *does.*

Give it some welly, man!

GEORGE *does it harder – grunts.*

ROSE. His mother says

DOCTOR. What?

GEORGE*'s* MOTHER *comes into the picture.*

MOTHER. Shell shock.

DOCTOR. Oh yes?

MOTHER. Look at him!

DOCTOR. I see.

MOTHER. It's his nerves.

ROSE. But that's all rot –

MOTHER. George?

ROSE. Isn't it, doctor?

MOTHER. Georgie?

ROSE. Doctor?

MOTHER. Georgie!

GEORGE (*confused*). Mother?

ROSE. It's what cowards say to get out of fighting:

DOCTOR. The term is 'war strain'.

GEORGE*'s* FATHER *comes into the picture*.

FATHER. George? It's your father.

DOCTOR. It's a blanket term.

FATHER. Can you hear me?

DOCTOR. It covers fatigue, loss of memory, anxiety,

GEORGE. Daddy!

DOCTOR. confusion, nightmares, tremors /

FATHER. 'Daddy'? You're a grown man, George!

DOCTOR. You're not very well are you?

GEORGE. I'm sorry.

DOCTOR. You don't need to be sorry.

FATHER. You need to pull yourself together, son.

DOCTOR. How is the marriage?

ROSE. Not easy.

FATHER. Be a man, George!

DOCTOR. Are you having… relations?

ROSE. Umm.

DOCTOR. Conjugals?

GEORGE. Yes!

ROSE. We do but… he finds it difficult. We both find it difficult. But we're *desperate* for a child. Aren't we, George?

GEORGE *says nothing*.

DOCTOR. I see.

ROSE. He spends all night alone walking the streets and all day sitting on the end of the bed staring out of the window. He says he's 'birdwatching'.

GEORGE. If it wasn't for the birds.

ROSE. Yes?

GEORGE. What hell it would be.

DOCTOR. Close your eyes for me, George.

GEORGE *does. The* DOCTOR *lifts a chair into the air, suspends it there and then drops it with a crash*. GEORGE *darts away cowering on the floor, terrified*.

**Lifeline 2**

*The scene continues from last Lifeline scene.*

FRANKIE. They stretched us too far. Had us pushing out to Malgir, setting up a new FOB there.

TONY. FOB?

FRANKIE. Forward Operating Base.

TONY. Oh yeah, right.

FRANKIE. But it's a shithole. No water, no electricity. Shitting in bags, sleeping in tents just feet from the burns pit. It's a hundred and forty degree heat! We're properly vulnerable. We're short of men. If we patrol we're at risk cos the terries way outnumber us. But if we don't patrol they'll get us surrounded and we're fucked. We complain and complain to the colonels and brigs, but they just say: 'We're winding down here. It's hearts and minds. Keep your cool.'

TONY. Helpful.

FRANKIE. Right! It's hard to keep your fucking cool when Taliban look just like civilians, right? The man and his kid crossing the field could be on their way to milk their cows or –

TONY. They could be on their way to end you.

FRANKIE. Yes! Paranoia means survival! And there's IEDs *everywhere*. You can't put one foot in front of the other without thinking, is this it? I still feel like that now, walking along the fucking seafront in Scarborough!

TONY. That's messed up.

FRANKIE. It gets you twisted. Up here. The heat and the hunger; we're living off rat packs cos they can't get fresh stuff through to us. Take away someone's food, someone's sleep and they become a completely different person.

TONY. Maybe that's when your true character comes out?

FRANKIE. Maybe. Maybe I am a monster. But they made me a monster! The army recruit you to kill. They condition you to kill. They expect you to kill. I was doing my job.

TONY. Yeah. Right. But…

FRANKIE. What?

TONY. There are rules, Frankie.

FRANKIE. Fuck the rules. Fuck the Geneva Convention.

TONY. Say that again?

FRANKIE. Fuck the Geneva Convention! You think they fight by the rules? There's this –

*He stops short.*

TONY. What?

FRANKIE. Forget it.

TONY. Go on, Frank.

FRANKIE. There's this little lad in our section that everyone calls Rusk, right? Cos his girlfriend sent him Farley's Rusks once in his care package, he just really liked them. And Rusk was green, you know, a proper crow. Any fucking mucky job we'd pass it on to Rusk cos that's the way it works. This is his first tour. And he's a ginger cunt too so… what does he expect?

One night he's sitting up on top of the ISO containers – thinks no one's around. And he's crying. Sobbing his heart out. I'm having a smoke down below with Taz who's this mental Welsh cage-fighter guy. Taz hears him and starts ripping the piss – I mean, really goes to town on him.

TONY. Poor bloke.

FRANKIE. Something snapped. Rusk jumps down and runs off, out past the sentry. Dead of night.

TONY. Shit.

FRANKIE. I tell Taz he's a *wanker*. Few minutes later we hear a bang.

We couldn't find much of him. Bits. We looked all night. Next morning…

TONY. Go on, mate.

FRANKIE. They'd… hung him. His leg. Arm. A bit of torso. Fucking… trophies. Hanging from this tree.

*Pause.*

I coulda been his mate. I was a runt on my first tour.

TONY *puts his hand on* FRANKIE*'s shoulder.* FRANKIE *pulls away, gets up, paces maybe.*

So yeah, we get wild! We get hungry. The smell of blood and shit and the heat and the flies and they've taken one of YOURS /

TONY. I totally get it, / mate

FRANKIE. You want *blood*. You can taste it. You wanna tear flesh off bones. Pop eyes out of sockets. Kick and kick until there's nothing / left!

TONY. You wanna kill! /

FRANKIE. You fucking do! /

TONY. They deserve it. /

FRANKIE. YES! /

TONY. You get off on it. /

FRANKIE. Yeah! What?

TONY (*getting animated, excited*). Our Darren said the moment he shot an insurgent in the chest he got hard. You ever had that?

FRANKIE. No.

TONY. Come on. You must have /

FRANKIE (*snapping*). Nah I haven't.

*Beat. Silence.*

But I know what you mean.

TONY. Yeah?

FRANKIE *sits down, glad to find someone who understands.*

FRANKIE. No one understands this shit. Sex and death are close. Killing. I'm not saying it's *sexual*, like. But the adrenalin. The release after. It feels like…

TONY. What?

FRANKIE. I don't know… like you've just… come or something.

*Beat. This really interests* TONY.

TONY. The thrill of killing?

FRANKIE. I guess.

TONY. Beating?

FRANKIE. 'Spose.

TONY. Your enemy?

FRANKIE. Yeah.

TONY. But he wasn't your enemy, was he?

FRANKIE. What?

TONY. He was just a poor little Afghan fuck.

*Beat.* FRANKIE *wonders what's happening.*

FRANKIE. We thought he was with them.

TONY. With who?

FRANKIE. The bastards who hung Rusk.

TONY. But he wasn't, was he?

FRANKIE. Look, if a soldier tells you to stop your bike, you stop your fucking bike. If he asks what you're doing, you tell him what you're doing – you don't just stand there and fucking smirk!

TONY. He'll never walk again /

FRANKIE (*spelling it out*). We thought he was Taliban!

TONY *stands up*.

TONY. Look, sorry, I'm not sure we can help.

FRANKIE. What?

TONY. We're not on the same wavelength like I thought. I better go, good luck and that.

TONY *begins to head off*. FRANKIE *gets in his way.* TONY *nods to a car in the distance*. FRANKIE *clocks it*.

FRANKIE. What you doing? Who's that?

TONY. Mate / look

*Beat. The penny drops.*

FRANKIE. Are you recording this? Your phone. 'Putting it on flight mode', you bastard. Gimme it.

*He makes a swipe for his top pocket*. TONY *darts away.*

TONY. Okay, Frankie, chill out, mate.

FRANKIE. I'm not your fucking mate.

*He lunges for him again.*

TONY. You see those lads by the Audi. They're my back-up.

FRANKIE *looks over, sees them. Stops.*

FRANKIE. You're press?

TONY. One of the Sundays. We'll run this tomorrow.

FRANKIE. I should fucking kill you!

*He makes one more lunge for him but he backs away.*

TONY. They're filming you, Frankie.

FRANKIE *stops.*

It's nothing personal, mate. Like you said, just doing my job.

TONY *leaves.* FRANKIE *is destroyed.*

## ACT THREE

### A Walk Around the Old Town

GEORGE. Rose is long asleep. Sneak out of the front door, slippers on my feet.

FRANKIE. Take the stairs two at a time. Check Mum's room; not there. Find my kit bag. Handfuls of clothes, shove them in.

NAT. Veer off the railway line before Pickering. Rest. But the seagulls swoop, almost grazing my head, telling me I'm on track, not to stop.

FRANKIE. Step into the shop and buy a bottle of vodka and throw away the lid. As I swig, it spills and stings my knuckles, grazed from punching a wall.

Early evening: high street's in limbo. Workers going home, drinkers going out.

GEORGE. Stand on the beach. Look out to sea. I dare them to come for me.

NAT. Come to a main road.

GEORGE. Follow the road round where the sea hugs the land. Hands stuffed in pockets.

NAT. Turn a corner and – neat rows of houses on the outskirts of town! Windows blown out and doors ripped off. You can hear a pin drop. And then –

FRANKIE *and* NAT. Peasholm Park.

NAT. The lake is covered with moss.

FRANKIE. A dad and his boy on the lake.

GEORGE. Can't let the thoughts set in. Can't let the dread in my head.

FRANKIE. And I run. Run like a kid tearing through back-of-his-hand streets. Just to feel the pavement slabs under my feet. The stone of home. I run until I reach

FRANKIE *and* NAT. The sea.

FRANKIE *and* NAT *both breathe. They both look out onto it. Sound of the sea. A moment.*

GEORGE. Up past the castle. Towards the Hill's Brow.

NAT. Take my shoes off. Dig my toes in the sand.

FRANKIE. Follow the road round where the sea hugs the land.

NAT. Write my name with a stick. Finn's name too.

FRANKIE. Reach the Castle. Run around the ruins. Drink.

GEORGE. The Hill's Brow – Look out over the town – Remember for a moment how Things Were Before. Turn, follow the shore, take the dark alleys home.

NAT. The castle is just as I left it! Just a few metres till the brow of the hill and then I'll see it:

FRANKIE. SCAR-BA-DOS!

NAT. Tear off

FRANKIE. Run up

NAT. Rucksack chafing.

FRANKIE. Trainers squelching.

FRANKIE *and* NAT. And I'm there.

*Beat. They both look out onto the view.* NAT *is in shock.*

FRANKIE. The old arcade and Luna Park rides. The chip shop and sweetshop. The rows upon rows of neat terraced housing. This town that has turned its back on me now.

NAT. And now *everything*… is obliterated.

FRANKIE. Oliver's Mount.

*Beat. Some time has passed.*

CHORUS. The War Memorial.

FRANKIE. I sit on the steps, neck my vodka.

CHORUS. Where he and Finn would have their imaginary battles
But

NAT. It's not there any more.
Just rocks, rubble.
Like a giant fist has punched at the earth
From the inside.

FRANKIE. I gaze up at the tower.
Makes my head spin.

NAT. And where it used to stand
Just a rugged and uneven stump.

FRANKIE (*reading*). 'And lo they passed over
and all the trumpets sounded for them
on the other side.
We will remember them – 1918.'

NAT. In the dust
There are shards of stone with letters – names of long-dead soldiers.

FRANKIE. Old-fashioned, English names.

NAT. I scrabble in the dirt. To find a name that makes sense.

FRANKIE. Potts, A.
Sharp, E.
Tibbs, R.
What was Tibbs like? Or Potts. Were they like me?
Or did they have dignity? Virtue?
What about Sharp? What did the E stand for? Edgar? Or… Elliot? Or Eric?

NAT. It's time.
Need to try to find… Finn.
Or what's left of him.
Possessions. Echoes. Stories.
Remains?

It rains and dirt turns to mud.
I scrabble and skid down the side of the hill.
Signposts gone, whole streets collapsed
So I make for the tiny stretch of sand.
Follow it round where the sea hugs the land.
The front I've strolled a thousand times
Shops blown out.
Their insides burned black.
Mangled and cracked coloured metal
From the VRcades
Litter the promenade.
And ragged grey-winged birds gather, pick pick picking away at…
A cage?
A ribcage.
A human ribcage. A corpse.
Run forward and fast; away

CHORUS. But his tablet bleeps, wakes from sleep
'Local connection detected'

NAT. 'Government Registry.' FUCK.

CHORUS. Not just net connection.
But the local area network
Information on all registered residents
And their whereabouts.

*There is a cacophony of pings and alert sounds.* NAT *can beam the contents of his tablet against a flat surface. 'Missing' alerts for civilians missing after the fighting. 'Wanted' alerts for members of the North Sea Alliance and other rebel groups. Fields are populated with 'Last seen wearing' 'Height age accent' 'Nickname.' 'Status'.*

NAT. The whole town is missing.

NAT *types his 'NATHANIAL AITKEN' name into the registry search. A picture of a young* NAT. *A 'Wanted' alert comes up. 'Reason: Failure to Serve. Desertion.' 'Status: Armed and dangerous – possibility.'* NAT *laughs at this. He closes his record before it has a chance to populate completely.*

NAT *nervously types 'FINN AITKEN' into the registry search. He holds his breath. A picture of picture of* FINN *looking older, mugshot maybe, more haggard and angry. 'Wanted' alert. 'Reason: Dissent.' 'Known associations: North Sea Movement.' 'Last seen: Scarborough Spa.'*

*Then it just flashes the word 'Populating' for a while (like buffering). It's agonising.*

*Then an alert ping and: 'RECORD UPDATED. STATUS: SUBJECT DECEASED'.*

*It flashes there for a while.*

Deceased.

CHORUS. Deceased.

NAT. Deceased.

CHORUS. Expired. Departed. Gone.

NAT. No more.

CHORUS. Nat falls to his knees. And the world stops turning.

Frankie lurches round the corner.
The world spins, then comes into focus.
And in front of him – The Lion.
(Crisps and Coke in the kids' room with Kayleigh.
Fingering Amy Shell in the toilets on New Year's.
A hundred lock-ins with the lads.)

FRANKIE. It's Saturday night
Sunday papers tomorrow.

CHORUS. Frankie stands on unsteady legs.
Drops his bottle
Spits in the gutter
And strides forward.

**The Lion**

RYAN *and* KET *are sitting at pub table.* LUKE *at the bar. They are in the pool room, and the main pub is busy and loud and 'Firestarter' by The Prodigy plays.* FRANKIE *hovers in the doorway – very nervous, thinks about bolting – then, after a few moments:*

RYAN (*loudly. Across the pub*). Well, *fuck* ME.

*All look towards* FRANKIE.

Little Frankie Musgrave! War hero of Scarbados!

RYAN *stands up. He's pissed and high on coke.*

Atten-TION! Left right, left right!

FRANKIE *doesn't move.* KET *laughs half-nervously.* RYAN *starts to march towards* FRANKIE *– comes face to face with him.*

What you doing here?

FRANKIE *shrugs.*

FRANKIE. Drink.

RYAN. You reckon you can drink here with us after what you've done?

LUKE. Ry–

RYAN. Shut up. Well, Musgrave. DO YA?

*Beat. Tension.*

FRANKIE. I'm sorry.

*As* FRANKIE *goes to bolt* RYAN *gets him in an affectionate headlock.* KET *runs over to greet him too.*

RYAN. HAHAHA! I'm joking, you fucking thick cunt.

KET. Alright, Frankie, / course he's joking

RYAN. Look at this clown's face! Thinks we don't wanna drink with him!

KET. Fucking classic. Mate!

KET *gives* FRANKIE *a bear hug.*

RYAN. Luke, look who it is:

LUKE *nods at* FRANKIE *from the bar. Cold.*

LUKE. Alright?

FRANKIE. Alright, Lukey.

RYAN. Get this man a drink.

*They sit at the table. Accelerated action of the night.*

FRANKIE. The pub. Ryan ain't slept for more than twenty-four hours; he's full of blow. I know that look. Eyes like saucers and breath that smells like bleach. Ket's tried to keep up but he's more pissed than anything. Used to be my sidekick, now he's Ryan's; hope he looks after him. Luke's quiet, just got back from fishing with his brothers, won't meet my eye. We sniff coke off a key when the barman's not there. It's like we're seventeen again, like I never left. The coke cuts through the vodka and I feel… amazing. My lager never tasted so crisp and so fine. These lads. *These lads*. They're mine.

RYAN. So we're meant to be going to Passion, right? And I meet this faggot at the bus station and he's only wearing a Black Sabbath T-shirt!

KET. It was the only one my mum washed.

RYAN. Your mum's a crackhead, mate. Black Sabbath! Black *jeans*, Frankie. DM boots. For *Passion*. I said why don't you go the whole hog, mate, put on some black lipstick, you gothic fuck.

FRANKIE. Did he get in?

RYAN. Did he bollocks.

KET. Ended up in Vivaz same as always.

*They laugh.*

RYAN. Here, they're looking for lads on the door, Frank. At Vivaz.

FRANKIE. Oh… right?

KET. Who'd wanna work there?

RYAN. What the fuck else is he gonna do? It's all Mad Paddy's done since leaving the army; door work – security. Can be a nice little earner if you don't mind getting your head kicked in now and then.

FRANKIE. We'll see.

*Beat.*

RYAN. Should have come last night, we tried to bell ya.

FRANKIE. Yeah my phone's fucked.

KET. And your mum said not to bother ya.

FRANKIE. Did she?

RYAN. Said you had a lot on your plate what with this court case coming up and that.

FRANKIE. You spoke to her?

RYAN. Fuck no. Your mum would rather eat dogshit than talk to me. That's what she told this dickhead.

KET. We've missed you, Frank.

RYAN. Soft prick.

KET. Nah, I mean – we think about you. Don't we?

RYAN. Yeah. I said, you wanna see Frankie's face nowadays you gotta buy *The* fucking *Sun*!

*They laugh.*

We're proud of ya, Musgrave.

FRANKIE (*taken aback*)…. Yeah?

KET. We are, Frank.

FRANKIE. Right.

RYAN. Yeah.

*They all take a swig of their drink. This is enormous for* FRANKIE *– a golden moment. Then – as* RYAN *puts his pint down:*

You give that little Osama a right good kicking.

*The air changes.*

FRANKIE. What?

RYAN. That'll learn the little Taliban cunt.

KET. His eyes was puffed up twice the size!

LUKE. He weren't Taliban, though, was he?

RYAN. They're all on the same side, Foster! And that ain't *our* side. Far as I'm concerned, you should have finished the job. He's a fucking hero, right? He's fought like a dog to protect us and our own. Here's to you, lad!

KET. To FRANKIE!

*Only* KET *and* RYAN *drink.*

RYAN. LUKE.

LUKE *drinks – reluctantly.*

LUKE. Frankie.

KET. Oi, the video's classic! You're an internet sensation.

RYAN (*impression of* FRANKIE). 'Want another one, do ya?'

KET. COME ON THEN CUNT!'

*They laugh.*

FRANKIE. Is that me?

KET. Yeah!

RYAN. 'That's it. Cry for Mummy!'

KET. 'Cry for your mummy, you little bitch!'/

FRANKIE. Stop it. I haven't seen it.

RYAN. Bollocks! /

FRANKIE. I haven't! /

RYAN. Oh, mate, you gotta watch it!

FRANKIE. No. I don't want to /

KET. It's ace – our Liam says you're a legend in his year! /

RYAN *is looking for it.*

FRANKIE. I'm not fussed. Let's get some shots, Jägers, yeah?

LUKE. Ryan –

RYAN. YES got it!

*He grabs for the phone but* RYAN *darts away.*

FRANKIE. Ryan /

RYAN. So funny. /

FRANKIE. Seriously. Don't.

RYAN. Fucking hell. There he is.

*He holds it out and it's just out of reach. The video plays and* FRANKIE *is frozen to the spot, transfixed, watching. Him beating, kicking repeatedly, shouting. It's really grotesque.* LUKE *looks away.* KET *and* RYAN *watch* FRANKIE *watching.* KET *touches* FRANKIE *on the shoulder.*

KET. Oi, Frankie /

FRANKIE *EXPLODES at* KET*'s touch – attacks him – headbutting him in the face.* RYAN *and* LUKE *have to drag* FRANKIE *off him. Mayhem.*

LUKE. Frank! What are you doing?

FRANKIE *runs.*

**George's Nightmare**

GEORGE. I creep in.
Undress and slide into bed
I lie as I do every night:
Stiff as a board, fists tight in a grip.
At my side Rose curls into me
I'm jealous of her easy slumber
This dumb animal.
And I wonder how I could have longed for her as I did.
I keep my breaths shallow and light
Afraid of what I what I might uncover
If I breathe too deep.
Afraid of my own heartbeat
I listen for the break of the waves
Will them to be gentle, rhythmic,
so my breaths can fall in time and I might
catch an hour or two
before I wake again; eyes-wide
no idea who I am or why I'm here.

But tonight, they're rough
I wince as each wave hits the sea wall.
Rears up and falls back.
I tense with each crash, each crack of water on stone
Is the snap of a rifle or a shell as it blows
I twist my body away from the window, wrestle the sheets
Damp with my sweat
They're coming for me
My men from the sea
The ghosts of the men
Who will not rise again
I breathe deep now and
fall
can't
help it
eyelids
heavy
caked with time and loss.

In a moist black hole where the air is filled with the sour
breath of eleven desperate men
CRASH a sea-spray white-light boom sends my brain
ricocheting around my skull
We are blown
We are thrown
Suspended for a moment then

Crash
On to hardened soil
Bones are shattered
Flesh is battered
Organs explode and
Faces blasted away

There's a warm body on me
The weight of another person
The heat of their skin
Rocks me then crushes me
Cradles then pushes
caresses then presses then
smooth taut skin against my face
ROSE?
(*Rubs his face as he did in previous scene with* ROSE.)
Rough grey chin and soft pink lips
TIBBS?
Turning cold then
Cold empty then
searching wet and hot and
gasping
Rose gasps breath
Tibbs' last breath
shudders out
as death sets in
NO
But now – life
My wife
There's cities of flesh
Between us
Fields of skin

she shushes me – and kisses me – and she's on top of me – and he's on top of me – no air in me – deadweight on me – she moves on me – puts me inside her – he's on top – she moves – he is heavy – there's no air – I can't breathe I can't breathe I can't breathe THERE'S NO AIR IN ME.

GEORGE *wakes and he is on top of* ROSE *– he has grabbed her by the throat in defence or is holding her down. She is terrified.*

**An Old Home**

NAT. The front door remains. The front two windows only cracked; boarded with cardboard and yellow newspaper. Above that, the whole upstairs side of the house – blown away.

My mother's bedroom; where she took her last breaths – the once-peach walls covered with grime and soot, the bed stripped, the dressing table on its side. A greying net curtain blows in the wind.

One push and the door gives way, swinging off one hinge. The hallway – damp and dark, the floorboards thick with dust.

The kitchen. Plates in the sink smeared with putrid food. I look for traces of super-hot chilli sauce – of Finn; nothing. The back wall gone. The half-room open to the elements. Vines spread over the ceiling – like nature trying to reclaim the house.

Back up the hall. I smooth my hand along the wall to reveal tiny copper leaves under a heavy layer of dust. I remember these. I stand at the foot of the stairs my heart in my throat – feel like I could vomit it…

Up… I tear at the stairs like I used to – two at a time, imagining them crumbling under my feet.

**A New Home**

GEORGE *is in a long thin room with lines of beds.* ROSE *and* DR COHAN *sit behind him. He has deteriorated. He speaks out, to the audience.*

GEORGE. There's a bird trapped behind my breastbone.
Trying to get out.
It flaps. Hurts.
Rattles around where my ribs make a cage
And makes me gulp for air.
Bigger than butterflies.
This is violence.

GEORGE *comes to sit in between* ROSE *and* DR COHEN. *He sits on his hands. Looks at the floor. And frequently rubs his face.*

ROSE. Have you shocked him?

COHEN. No.

ROSE. I mean, I hate to think of it, but if it makes him / better

COHEN. We don't do that any more.

ROSE. Well, what do you do, doctor?

COHEN. We… talk.

ROSE. Talk??

GEORGE (*mumbling*). Grey face. Pink lips.

ROSE. Does he even know who I am?

GEORGE. No air.

ROSE. He's worse than when he was admitted!

GEORGE (*as though coming to*). Rose.

ROSE. Yes! Rose.

GEORGE *laughs a bit.*

GEORGE. Got fat.

ROSE. George!

COHEN. He's disinhibited, / he doesn't –

ROSE. I am not *fat*, George – / I'm

COHEN. Don't. Mrs Hollins – you'll confuse him.

TIBBS *enters. Sits down next to* GEORGE. *They start to play Scissors, Paper, Stone.* GEORGE *becomes distracted, only interested in his friend.* GEORGE *likes having him there and it keeps his attention from their conversation. To* ROSE *and* DR COHEN, *he appears in his own world.*

ROSE. There! He's off again! What is he *doing*, doctor?

COHEN. Did you ever talk to George about the war?

ROSE. No, absolutely not. And if he ever brought it up I'd change the subject.

COHEN. Did he bring it up often?

ROSE. Sometimes. I told him he must put it out of his mind. That's right, isn't it?

COHEN. It may seem… illogical, but no.

ROSE. No?

COHEN. A soldier is trained to repress feelings. To react in a calm, methodical way in traumatic situations. How could they get through war otherwise?

ROSE. Quite.

COHEN. And that repression continues after war. When they come home. They repress ugly violent memories so they can get on with their lives. With their wives, their families.

ROSE. But he can't get on with his life. Look at him!

COHEN. That's because it doesn't work! We see now. It doesn't work.

ROSE. I don't understand.

COHEN. It comes back; the trauma. In nightmares and flashbacks and fears and anxieties. All sorts of physical manifestations. George's tics. I have men who can't walk! Who can't see, can't speak!

ROSE (*scoffing*). Can't *walk* because of… memories?

COHEN. Now we advocate *confronting* these memories. Working through them. We've had some excellent results.

ROSE *stands*.

ROSE. I think we should find somewhere else for George to be seen.

COHEN. This is pioneering treatment, Mrs Hollins /

ROSE. I need to see more progress than this, doctor! A more… vigorous regimen. George! /

COHEN. Of course. Maybe you'd prefer he *was* shocked. His mouth forced open, a strong faradic current applied to the pharynx? Or screamed at for hours? Exposed to violent situations?

ROSE (*horrified*). Of course not! I just… want him back!

ROSE *breaks a little and* GEORGE *glances over to her. Their eyes meet.*

COHEN (*gently*). He's sleeping better. Dreaming less.

ROSE *softens a little with regret.*

ROSE. So if I had let him talk – when he cried out in the night for me, if I hadn't turned away, then we wouldn't be where we are?

COHEN. It's not that simple. He needs medical care.

ROSE. What would he have said to me?

COHEN. Maybe he would have told you what he told me.

ROSE. Which was?

DOCTOR. He was at Pilckem Ridge in July, 1917.

*As though* GEORGE *is telling* COHEN – *not in real time.*

GEORGE. Me and the boys in an abandoned dugout. Hiding for hours – rain. Guns jammed with the mud. Up to our knees in it. We share the last of our fags and talk about old schooldays and what our sweethearts would be up to. Then this fearful crash. We're blown to blazes. It goes black. And I wake... with my friend lying heavy on top of me. Tibbs. I talk to him but he doesn't talk back because he's dead. They're all dead. Eric and Potts and Robbie... All of them. But there we stay... together. Days. The smell of them. My foot leaking blood, waiting for the gangrene. My darkest days on this earth. But for the birds; hawfinches. A crested lark. Thrushes. And a robin: a little glimpse of home.

DOCTOR. He was found, rescued, some days later.

*Beat.*

ROSE. Will he get better? Can he?

COHEN. I'm confident he will improve.

ROSE. But, will he be *my* George again?

COHEN. Mrs Hollins... I –

ROSE. I want to know. I want to...

*She turns to* GEORGE.

George. I want to...

**Reunion**

*An exhausted-looking, haggard* FINN.

FINN. I want to return to my home
I want to climb into my bed
Pull the covers over
Let the dark take me
And in the night; rewind the time
Clear the years
So when I wake
The house is clean, the walls intact
And I'm a boy again;
My voice high, my body soft and thin.
I want the smell of toast and frying eggs and coffee
The radio on low, my mother singing
My brother filling the bathroom with steam and smells.
I want to play for the day
Not have to run or hide, frightened of shadows
Computer games or hockey or
The VRcades with Nat!
I want to forget the world

I want to return to my home.
I need to return to my home.
I lurk in alleyways.
Cut through parks.
Make myself invisible.
Until

I'm on the other side of the front door, still.
Taking a breath. Taking it in.
Haven't been back for months.
Straight up the stairs, make a beeline for my room.
Where I can rest my head and lick my wounds
But outside the door
I sense movement, noise
Grab the knife from my shoe, poised
Ready to defend

Inside the room a hooded figure bends down by the bed
Staring at the skirting where my brother and I scratched our initials
And 'New Year's Eve 2020' – the start of a new decade.
I'm filled with territorial rage
I grab him around the neck
Drag him backwards
He grabs at me
Shouts
Swears
We wrestle and we kick
And as we take a dive
And I have one word in my head
'Survive.'
And as I drive the knife into his side.
His hood falls back.

**Transitions**

FRANKIE. I run from The Lion to the shore. Coming down off the coke now, so no more Billy Big Bollocks. I just feel fucking sad. Sad for Ket, he didn't mean any harm and I broke his nose. Sad for Rusk the newbie with his limbs hanging in the trees and for Badrawi Kabir, whose name means 'Beautiful, radiant' and who will never walk again, because of me.

Sad for Mum, when she reads tomorrow about her monster son. Sad for Kayleigh, and Jenson and Nan – their Scarborough war hero told the world he feels like he comes when he kills a man. Sad for the man I could have been.

I take my shoes off. Ice-cold sea on white feet. Taste blood. Squat. Sand in my fists, wind in my hair, spit blood in the water. Blood and sand and the salt of my tears and the sea.

I howl at the sky and roar at the waves: SAVE ME OR FUCKING DESTROY ME.

I want to be the waves.

I want something to change.
I want all this pain to make the sky turn red.
Or crack the surface of the earth.
Watch the sea wall lashed
Watch the waves swallow the cars and the houses and the people on their sofas watching telly, in their bedrooms making love.

But nothing changes, there is nothing except the dark forever.

But there. A light? A light… A light!

A tiny boat far out to sea. Where are you going? Can you take me?

FINN. A face I know. As the knife reaches its hilt in his flesh his blue eyes open wide, connect with mine. As I start to pull the knife out, time stops. Life replays. I see him as I saw him last, red-faced and shouting, waving arms as the boat speeds away. And I wade towards him, pointlessly, knowing… he can't swim.

I pull the knife out a little more, and I'm back roaming the streets, Nat gone. Wondering how I'll go on without him. Frantic messages and calls from him. Missing school cos I can, doing errands for the North Sea gang who take me under their wing, feed me, call me 'The Boy'. Teach me how to shoot a gun. Another inch out and I'm in training. Four hours sleep a night. Sweat. Hunger. Camaraderie. I take no more calls from Nat. I tell him I have no brother now. Although I do – I have thousands.

Another inch and I'm back at The Spa, wedged under the window frame shooting for hours. The smell of decaying bodies. Being dragged out by government forces. Rotting in a shipping container with four other rebels – all staunch and true men – stronger than me. *They* won't answer their questions, no matter what they do to them.

But I do. I do. Because… fear. Because pain. And now I'm no rebel. I'm a rat. I buckle under the brutality of it all.

The knife is fully out and my brother falls and I catch him in my arms.

GEORGE. I walk. I follow a woman with a candle. Our footsteps and the jangle of keys and hushed voices. Is it dawn? Long windows line the halls and dark-green vines creep in spreading like tentacles across the ceiling. A man at my side, clutches my elbow.

Am I dreaming? If I'm dreaming then where is the blood? Where is the mud where are my grey-faced men? Where's my little bird? Light from the candle casts tall shadows on the wall. A ghostly trio trudging forever forward. Is this my death? Will I be shot at dawn?

Corners and keys and corridors. Corners and keys and corridors. I falter. The man tightens his grip. Eric, Tibbs, I'm for it, lads – Court Martial or worse! I'll see you soon…

No more windows. No light at the end. And there's… screaming; piercing, reverberating in my chest. I drop to the floor – but they pull me up.
And we walk, the screaming ringing in my ear
We walk and we walk our footsteps heavy and clear
Walk
Walk walk
This is it
This is the end
She opens the door and

Rose.
*My* Rose.
If she's here then heaven it is.
But she's been crying.
Lying in a hospital bed!
'What have they done to you, my love?'

And she passes me a bundle of rags.
Says 'He's yours, George.'

*Pause.*

'He's yours.'

FRANKIE. Tiny light on the dark sea

GEORGE. Tiny red face, warm pink flesh

NAT. Finn.

FINN. Don't speak.

NAT. You're here!

FINN. I didn't know who you were. Shhh.

FRANKIE. I wade forward
Grit my teeth against the cold

FINN. I tell him we'll wait for dawn.
As soon as it's first light
We'll take flight. Get help

FRANKIE. I've trained for this:
Brave the waves

FINN. We'll go for help
I hold my T-shirt to his wound
There's hope. There's hope

GEORGE. His swaddling falls away
And all that's left is this little life

FRANKIE. Give myself to the water

GEORGE. In my hands

FINN. Rest.

FRANKIE. To the darkness

FINN. Breathe.

GEORGE. Life

FINN. I hold him like he held me
The night my mum died
He calls for her. And for me. And a name I don't recognise:

NAT. Elias.

FRANKIE. I'm moving on

FINN. I hold him

FRANKIE. I'm getting out

FINN. I rock him as he cries

FINN *and* GEORGE. He cries

FINN. In his hand; a hairpin. A button. A small plastic car.

FRANKIE. I can swim that far.

NAT. Brother.

FINN. You're home now.

NAT. I can –

FINN. Wait for the light,

GEORGE. His flesh on my flesh

FRANKIE. I can

GEORGE. My flesh

FINN. For the dawn.

GEORGE. His flesh

FRANKIE. I can swim

NAT. Brother.

FRANKIE. I can swim to the light

FINN. His eyes still open.

FRANKIE. I can

FINN. The world still turns.

FRANKIE. I can swim
I can swim
I can
(*Gasps.*)
I

*Beat.*

GEORGE. I hold him up to the light.
And I think: a beginning.
Yes.
A beginning.

*End.*

**Other Titles in this Series**

Mike Bartlett
ALBION
BULL
GAME
AN INTERVENTION
KING CHARLES III
WILD

Tom Basden
THE CROCODILE
HOLES
JOSEPH K
THERE IS A WAR

Andrew Bovell
SPEAKING IN TONGUES
THINGS I KNOW TO BE TRUE
WHEN THE RAIN STOPS FALLING

Jez Butterworth
THE FERRYMAN
JERUSALEM
JEZ BUTTERWORTH PLAYS: ONE
MOJO
THE NIGHT HERON
PARLOUR SONG
THE RIVER
THE WINTERLING

Caryl Churchill
BLUE HEART
CHURCHILL PLAYS: THREE
CHURCHILL PLAYS: FOUR
CHURCHILL: SHORTS
CLOUD NINE
DING DONG THE WICKED
A DREAM PLAY *after* Strindberg
DRUNK ENOUGH TO SAY I LOVE YOU?
ESCAPED ALONE
FAR AWAY
HERE WE GO
HOTEL
ICECREAM
LIGHT SHINING IN BUCKINGHAMSHIRE
LOVE AND INFORMATION
MAD FOREST
A NUMBER
SEVEN JEWISH CHILDREN
THE SKRIKER
THIS IS A CHAIR
THYESTES *after* Seneca
TRAPS

Fiona Doyle
ABIGAIL
COOLATULLY
DELUGE
THE STRANGE DEATH OF JOHN DOE

Vivienne Franzmann
BODIES
MOGADISHU
PESTS
THE WITNESS

Stacey Gregg
LAGAN
OVERRIDE
PERVE
SCORCH
SHIBBOLETH
WHEN COWS GO BOOM

Sam Holcroft
COCKROACH
DANCING BEARS
EDGAR & ANNABEL
PINK
RULES FOR LIVING
THE WARDROBE
WHILE YOU LIE

Anna Jordan
CHICKEN SHOP
FREAK
POP MUSIC
YEN

Dawn King
CIPHERS
FOXFINDER

Lucy Kirkwood
BEAUTY AND THE BEAST *with* Katie Mitchell
BLOODY WIMMIN
CHIMERICA
HEDDA *after* Ibsen
IT FELT EMPTY WHEN THE HEART WENT AT FIRST BUT IT IS ALRIGHT NOW
LUCY KIRKWOOD PLAYS: ONE
MOSQUITOES
NSFW
TINDERBOX

Sam Potter
HANNA

Stef Smith
GIRL IN THE MACHINE
HUMAN ANIMALS
REMOTE
SWALLOW

Jack Thorne
2ND MAY 1997
BUNNY
BURYING YOUR BROTHER IN THE PAVEMENT
A CHRISTMAS CAROL *after* Dickens
HOPE
JACK THORNE PLAYS: ONE
JUNKYARD
LET THE RIGHT ONE IN *after* John Ajvide Lindqvist
MYDIDAE
THE SOLID LIFE OF SUGAR WATER
STACY & FANNY AND FAGGOT
WHEN YOU CURE ME
WOYZECK *after* Büchner

**A Nick Hern Book**

*The Unreturning* first published in Great Britain in 2018 as a paperback original by Nick Hern Books Limited, The Glasshouse, 49a Goldhawk Road, London W12 8QP, in association with Frantic Assembly and Theatre Royal Plymouth



Cover image: Hugo Glendinning

Designed and typeset by Nick Hern Books, London
Printed and bound in Great Britain by CPI Group (UK) Ltd

A CIP catalogue record for this book is available from the British Library

ISBN 978 1 84842 787 7



FSC www.fsc.org MIX Paper from responsible sources FSC® C013604